W9-BZB-740

WOMEN'S GUIDE TO FINANCIAL SELF-DEFENSE

WOMEN'S GUIDE TO FINANCIAL SELF-DEFENSE

JUNE MAYS

WARNER BOOKS

A Time Warner Company

If you purchase this book without a cover you should be aware that this book may have been stolen property and reported as "unsold and destroyed" to the publisher. In such case neither the author nor the publisher has received any payment for this "stripped book."

The vignettes in this book represent composites of many different women whom the author has known during her financial career; resemblance to any one actual person is purely coincidental.

Every effort has been made to give helpful advice, but no warranty against financial loss is given by the author or publisher. As laws and practices often vary from state to state, the reader is advised to consult with a professional regarding specific decisions.

Copyright © 1997 by June Mays
All rights reserved.

Warner Books, Inc., 1271 Avenue of the Americas, New York, NY 10020
Visit our Web site at
http://pathfinder.com/twep

W A Time Warner Company

Printed in the United States of America
First Printing: April 1997
10 9 8 7 6 5 4 3 2 1

Library of Congress Cataloging-in-Publication Data

Mays, June.
    Women's guide to financial self-defense / June Mays.
      p. cm.
    Includes bibliographical references (p.).
    ISBN 0-446-67264-5
      1. Women—Finance, Personal. 2. Divorced women—Finance,
Personal. 3. Windows—Finance, Personal. I. Title.
HG179.M3734 1997
332.024'042—dc20   96-20081
                                        CIP

Book design and text composition by L&G McRee
Cover design by Christine Van Bree
Cover photo by Herman Estevez

ATTENTION: SCHOOLS AND CORPORATIONS
WARNER books are available at quantity discounts with bulk purchase for educational, business, or sales promotional use. For information, please write to: SPECIAL SALES DEPARTMENT, WARNER BOOKS, 1271 AVENUE OF THE AMERICAS, NEW YORK, N.Y. 10020.

Acknowledgments

Thanks to Jordan Ball, Rick Beiswenger, Betty Broome, Judy Crittenden, Ken Crowe, Jane Gaston, Rusty and Carolyn Goldsmith, Kim Harless, Paul Homan, Bob Mann, Joe Mays, Bill McLemore, Ron Meredith, Kathryn Miree, Wilmer Poyner, Rainer Twiford, Ralph Yeilding, Dolly Young, and to many women who were kind enough to share their stories. Thanks to my clients who tested the notebook in our "Getting It Together" seminars.

Contents

Author's Note

Are you a woman who would like to know more about the family finances, but your husband is reluctant to share financial information? If so,

THIS BOOK IS FOR YOU; READ ON.

Are you a busy wife with volunteer activities, children, or a career? Perhaps you welcome the fact that your husband is willing to take care of the money and feel you are smart enough to pick up the reins and manage the family finances should death, divorce, or disability strike. If so,

THIS BOOK IS FOR YOU; READ ON.

Are you a woman who has fallen into an easy routine of allowing your husband to handle money? You know you'll be in trouble when death, divorce, or disability comes. If so,

THIS BOOK IS FOR YOU; READ ON.

Are you a man who wants to encourage and assist his wife or mother to get financially organized? If so,

THIS BOOK IS FOR YOU; READ ON.

Are you a woman who is frightened of money? When your husband starts talking about the family finances, do you cover your ears and leave the room? If so,

THIS BOOK IS FOR YOU; READ ON.

Are you a woman who can handle money but feels a need to be more organized? If so,

THIS BOOK IS FOR YOU; READ ON.

WOMEN'S
GUIDE TO
FINANCIAL
SELF-DEFENSE

Introduction

ONE BILLION DOLLARS. Lay a stack of that many dollar bills flat and it would reach around the world four times. That's the amount of assets reported in 1994 as abandoned.* It's much more now. While the fate of this money varies among states, all of these assets have come from bank accounts or other liquid assets lost by their original owners. Some were even advertised publicly and still not claimed. Why were these assets abandoned? My guess is that a significant portion belonged to people who for different reasons didn't tell anyone about them, possibly forgot about them, and then died. One billion dollars is a lot of money to take out of use by individuals. Missing assets could mean the difference between survival and comfort for a deceased person's family.

Not only bank accounts, but also insurance policies are forgotten. Off the top of your head—right now—can *you*

*National Association of Unclaimed Property Administrators

name all *your* insurance policies and who is to benefit? Are you sure? Could someone other than you find these policies?

In my career as an investment broker, I have seen widows in confusion and fear because they felt they did not have enough money to live on. These women would be grateful to know about missing bank accounts and insurance benefits.

I have seen women struggle to make ends meet, only to discover there was plenty of money all along in places they never knew. I have seen estates reopened at substantial expense because stray stock certificates and bonds turned up. I have seen families live in bitterness over misunderstandings on disposal of a deceased person's assets. I have seen divorced women taken advantage of because they did not know about existing family finances until it was too late.

A woman for whom everything is going well can be left, in a matter of hours, with a severely disabled or paralyzed husband who cannot tell her all the things he had been intending to tell her.

Do you see yourself in the future as an uninformed widow, divorcee, or spouse in charge? Because of death, divorce, or disability of your spouse, the chances are great that you will be left to handle the finances yourself. Now— while you and your spouse are still alive, well, and communicating—is the time to do something about it. You may be capable and sophisticated, but if you are uninformed, there may be a disaster waiting to happen. Now is the time for you to attend to your own financial self-defense.

The first part of this book relates stories of women who were uninformed and then gives advice that might prevent a similar fate for you.

The next section of the book is "Your Notebook," a day-by-day, step-by-step guide to financial organization in thirty days. Your notebook, a collection of financial information about your family, will save you hours of frustration when you are left to make decisions and to act on your own.

The last section will provide you with strategies for your financial self-defense and with information you will need to understand your financial accounts, your investments, your insurance, and your long-term financial future.

DON'T LET THIS HAPPEN TO YOU

Sharon

"We seemed to have plenty. My husband always gave me money each month for maid service, dry cleaning, utilities, club dues, and pocket money. Anything else I wanted I charged, and he paid. I never questioned him. I had no idea what bad shape he was in until he filed for bankruptcy."

What could Sharon have done to prevent this from happening?

*She could have questioned her husband about their financial affairs. Together they could have taken a backward look at how they spent their income, **even if it appeared they did not need a budget.** That examination would no doubt have brought to light their cash flow problem, hopefully in time to do something about it. When things seem to be going well, it can be hard to "rock the boat." As you can see from what happened to Sharon, sometimes the boat needs rocking.*

Sharon could have set up an investment account for herself in her own name and funded it from her monthly allowance. After her husband's bankruptcy, she would have had something to call her own.

5

Martha

"When I began to question him about money, he replied, 'You don't need to know that. . . . My job is to take care of you. . . . You've got a vivid imagination. . . . You've been watching too many soap operas.' When I signed the tax return, he cupped his hand over the amount of income so I couldn't see how much he made. Whenever he said, 'Sign these papers,' I always signed them. Later, when I said I wouldn't sign, he forged my name. When we separated and he left, he refused to make payments on our house. He canceled all his life insurance naming me as beneficiary. Even though I had left my bearer bonds in the safekeeping department of my bank with a signed note that my bonds were not to be pledged, our banker—*his friend*—accepted my bearer bonds as collateral on my husband's loan. When my husband defaulted, I lost my bonds. I owned stock in his corporation and had loaned his company some money. When I asked for copies of the tax returns of the corporation, his CPA said I couldn't have them without a release from the president, my husband." (Author's note: The law in most states says that any stockholder who owns 5 percent or more of a business is entitled to see all financial records.)

"After the separation he came back and robbed our house. I know it was him because only the things covered by the insurance rider were taken and because the cat was left locked in the basement the way my husband always left him. He sold the gold coins and jewelry that he had stolen. Then he tried to get money from the insurance claim!

"After the divorce the court said he had to pay me $2,000 a month property settlement until all he had taken from me had been repaid. He immediately filed for bankruptcy, which I had overturned because of fraud. All this cost me: I had to pay the lawyer 50 percent of what was recovered, $6,000 to the accountant, $15,000 to the divorce attorney, plus fees and filing expenses. When he filed bankruptcy the court reduced my property settlement to $400 a month. And now I have to garnish him for that.

"My advice to all women is to find out all you can about your husband's business, especially if you are a part owner or have loaned him money. Read everything you sign. Have a banker you know and trust."

Good words of advice from Martha! Things could have turned out much better if she had gotten to know her banker, if she had spent time learning about the family business, and if she had read the documents she was given to sign.

What else could Martha have done to prevent these things from happening to her?

She could have spent more time at the family business, serving as a part-time receptionist, file clerk, or assistant. That way she would have been in touch with customers, would have been able to review the financial files and become familiar with daily operations. Taking an interest in the business could have been a career generator for Martha and an asset to the corporation. She might have discovered that her loan to the corporation could have been repaid before it was too late.

She could have made and kept a copy of each year's tax return. After all, she did sign it. Later she could study the return to see how much money they were making and from what sources, how much interest they were paying and to whom. A tax return can also give you clues to how much money there is. For example, if you show interest earned of $10,000 and short-term rates are 5 percent, then you must have approximately $200,000 out there earning interest somewhere.

Martha could have prepared a net worth statement for herself and her husband, as you will learn to do later in this book. If she had, she would have known how much debt was in place and in whose name the assets were owned.

Although it may seem ruthless, particularly to the newly married, Martha would have been in better shape if she had kept more of her property in her name. You don't want to wind up like Martha, with a promise to repay her for assets stolen but then left empty-handed by her husband's bankruptcy.

If Martha had kept most of her property in a form that couldn't be tampered with, she could have preserved it from being sold by her husband. Having your net worth mostly in bearer bonds, gold coins, jewelry, collections, silver, and the like, which can be sold by anyone, is not a good idea.

Martha could have deposited her bearer bonds in an investment account at a bank or brokerage, where there would have been safeguards against the release of her bonds. If she had confirmed annually with her bank the inventory of the bonds she had left in their safekeeping, the theft of the bonds would have come to light a lot earlier.

Dorothy

"When Bob had his stroke and was in the rehab hospital for so long, it was really hard on me to piece everything together. He couldn't talk. He couldn't sign his name. I found enough money to pay the bills, but later, when notices of maturing CDs from different banks around town arrived in the mail, I was furious that he hadn't told me about them before his stroke. I would have felt a lot easier. It took me one year to get everything straight, and our affairs are not that complicated."

What could Dorothy have done to prevent this state of affairs?

She could have taken as her responsibility the collection of data for the annual tax return. That would have told her where the CDs were. She could have kept a notebook in which she filed bank statements and replaced them once a year.

Dorothy and her husband could have had durable powers of attorney drawn up by their lawyer. In the event one became incapacitated, the other could act on his or her behalf.

Mary

"After John died I was afraid to answer the phone, afraid to open the mail. There were reams and reams of paper. I had no idea how to fill out all the forms I was sent. It was just unbelievable to me. During the first year, the most difficult aspect of my widowhood was handling my business affairs. I was completely ignorant of how to do it. Now I believe every woman should *know how* to handle the family finances, even if she doesn't assume primary responsibility for them."

What could Mary have done to avoid being overcome by the financial deluge that hit her?

Paying the bills or at least reading the bills could have been a real eye-opener. Being familiar with the financial mail that comes in could have reduced Mary's anxiety.

Preparing a retroactive statement of the family expenses over a six-month period would have prepared her for what to expect. There are some excellent computer programs that make this a lot easier than the old "by hand" method. By reconstructing how her family spent its money the last six months, not only would she have had a good idea of the cash outflow—she would have taken a step toward budgeting for the future.

Mom

"For months after Dad died, Mom found money around the house—under the bed, in books, in bowls, behind the clock. She found his Rolex in a Pepto-Bismol box in the medicine cabinet."

What could Mom have done?

*As her husband became eccentric, afflicted by memory disorders or exhibited bizarre behavior, she could have stopped leaving cash lying around in accessible spots. Perhaps she could have prevented some of the hoarding by throwing away and giving away the clutter that elderly people seem to accumulate, **always checking the boxes and the drawers first!***

It is so easy to tune out on the talk of elderly people; if Mom had really paid attention to what her husband was saying, even when he seemed to make no sense, she might have picked up on some of his secrets.

Cathy

"Mother is a very smart woman, but she knows nothing about her finances. She never writes checks. She has never reconciled a bank statement. Daddy always handles everything. He never tells her about their accounts because she doesn't want to know. I don't know what she'll do when Daddy gets sick or dies."

It is hard to believe there are women who don't know how to write checks—but it is very true, and you may be one of them. Cathy needs to have a serious talk with her mother and her father while both are still living and functioning. Cathy could tell them how important it is to her for her mother to feel at ease with the family finances. Cathy should say that her mother doesn't have to take over anything, just understand *what she and Cathy's father have and what Cathy's father does on a daily basis to handle the couple's finances.*

If Cathy gave her mother a copy of this book and volunteered to help her get started assembling a notebook (see page 39), perhaps her mother would be more likely to gather the information needed. Gathering this information will make Cathy's mother much more comfortable now and *in the future.*

Cathy's mother should spend a half hour with her branch bank officer, learning to write a check, to balance a checkbook, and to read a bank statement. Cathy's mother should not be embarrassed; people who work in bank branches are trained to be helpful and nonjudgmental.

Sally

"I'm the second wife. I know he's never changed the beneficiary on his life insurance policies. I know if he dies, his first wife gets the death benefits. I've asked him to take care of it, but he keeps putting it off. What can I do?"

It should be obvious to Sally that her husband still feels protective of his first wife; he is not going to change the beneficiary on the policy. Sally should accept that and take out a new policy on her husband's life that she owns and controls and of which she is the beneficiary. Many men who have had amicable divorces and who have children from the earlier marriage feel obligated to leave existing life insurance in place.

Susan

"My husband was killed in an automobile accident. I had paid the bills; all he did was deposit his paychecks. I knew how to handle money, but with no gainful employment or personal credit history, I was denied a credit card. Every account was in his name."

What could Susan have done to have been allowed a credit card?

She could have made sure the credit card accounts were not just in her husband's name, but in joint name. That way, she would have been building her credit history along with her husband. When he died the account would have become hers automatically. If you can, have your own credit card or make sure the one you are using is joint.

If she knew her banker and had some form of collateral, perhaps she could have taken out a small personal loan and repaid it to establish a credit history.

Finding herself without a credit card after her husband died, she could have opened a securities account with a brokerage firm that offered a debit card as part of the package; no credit history is required.

Elizabeth

"Before we divorced, my husband called our young and inexperienced investment broker. My husband told him to close the money-market funds in his account and in my account. My husband knew he would not be able to pick up my check in person without written instructions in hand from me, so he asked the broker to mail the checks. The broker did it. My husband intercepted the checks and deposited them both in his own account. I got the money back in the divorce settlement, but it took several months."

What could Elizabeth have done to prevent the broker from taking her husband's instructions regarding her account?

If she suspected that her husband might do something like this, she could have made a point of telling her broker never to take orders from her husband regarding her account without first confirming with her. In the past, if a broker dealt consistently with only one spouse, this type of thing would have been more likely to happen. These days, every broker should be aware of the privacy of single-name accounts.

Nancy

"Sam and I were married for ten wonderful years. We thought his will was foolproof. We never thought his adopted stepchildren from his first marriage would contest his will, much less break it, but they did."

What could Nancy and Sam have done to prevent this from happening?

They could have met with a good estate attorney in their city and, having briefed the attorney on their past family histories, asked if the will could be broken. An attorney cannot prevent a will being contested but should be able to construct a will so the wishes of the deceased can be fulfilled. Meeting with the estate attorney would have been even more important if Sam and Nancy had moved to another state of residence since their wills were written. Meeting with an estate attorney would have been important if it had been five or more years since Sam and Nancy had had their wills reviewed.

Joann

"I was so frightened; I didn't think I should trust anyone. You know the stories of old people falling for scams; I was afraid other people would take me to the cleaners. I needed more income, but I was afraid to move money out of my checking account. I'm okay now, but it would have been much better for me if I had known about investments before my husband died and I was left alone."

What could Joann have done to alleviate her fears?

Before her husband died, while he was still functioning at 100 percent, they could have done a projection of cash flow after her husband's death. If it did not appear to be sufficient, she and her husband could have met with their broker, financial planner, or banker to discuss income investments Joann might choose in the future.

This is particularly important if current sources of income will cease in the future or with the death of the spouse. Many widows have been surprised by pension income that disappeared with the death of a spouse.

*If Joann had been in contact with her banker, financial planner, or broker before her husband's death, perhaps she would have felt more trusting or **would have known ahead of time that she would not be comfortable on her own with that individual and would have sought other counsel.** There is no law that says you have to use the same banker, broker, or financial planner your spouse used.*

Anything Joann could have done to have felt more accustomed to dealing with the family finances would have been helpful, such as reviewing the monthly brokerage statements and bank statements or breaking down the expenditures into categories.

Alice

"I know some people would call me rich, but I don't feel that way. When Bill was alive I never had to live on a budget; I was able to get whatever I wanted. Now that Bill's gone, how much money can I spend without using up all my money? How much income should I expect to make from my investments? I wish we had talked about this before my husband died."

Alice is right. If she and Bill had discussed the "what if's," she would have been better prepared for handling the money on her own.

What else could Alice have done to feel more comfortable?

If she had constructed a budget during normal times, even though she didn't seem to need one, she would have had a good idea of what her expenses would be after Bill died.

If she was accustomed to reviewing their brokerage statements and CDs, she would have known where to look on the statement to determine the expected income from her investments.

Catherine

"Mom and Dad were very smart. They had their estate attorney draw wills so their assets would go into trusts upon their deaths. But they never got around to changing the title on their assets from joint to single names. So when Dad died there was nothing to put into his trust; and Mom was so panicky, she wouldn't renounce claim to $600,000 so it could go into the trust, even though the lawyer explained to her that she would continue to have the income. Dad's unified credit was lost. That means when Mom dies, we will have to pay estate tax on $600,000 that we could have avoided."

What could Catherine's mom and dad have done to have prevented this unnecessary turn of events? Having gone two-thirds of the way, they could have completed the estate planning task by making the necessary transfers of assets into their single names, as instructed by their attorney. This could have taken as little as five minutes to complete.

Barbara

"Dad was in such a state when Mother died. And when I look back on it, we didn't help matters much. Dad didn't know what to do with Mother's ring, and she hadn't left any instructions for him. It was beautiful. It had five stones— because she had five children. We squabbled so much over it that Dad finally took the ring to the jeweler, had the stones removed, and gave one stone to each of us. Now the beautiful ring is gone and the stones are so small, they are really useless."

What could Barbara's mother have done to prevent this family strife?

She could have made notes, signed and dated, on the disposition of her personal property before she died. This would have given her an opportunity to make an equable distribution or to make special bequests. You will have an opportunity to do this yourself when you construct your notebook later.

Laura

"I just can't take this anymore!" The recently widowed, distinguished scientist's chin quivered as she dropped into the chair in my office. "I just left my husband's company, where I went to ask about his benefits. I was passed around until I wound up with the person I started with. They were so rude, and it took one hour and twenty minutes. I'd rather have been working in the lab."

What could Laura have done to have made dealing with the system easier?

She could have made a phone call rather than a visit. Phone calls take less time. Have you ever been waiting in line at a counter while the helper took phone calls and left you standing there? Whether we like it or not, the customer on the phone often gets the best treatment. If Laura felt she wasn't being treated properly, she could always hang up and try again without taking too much of her time. She could have written down her questions before she made the phone call.

These stories didn't have to happen. In my career I have had to help many women like these and deal with these events. Don't let stories like these happen to you. Defend yourself financially! The next section—"Your Notebook"—will provide you with a tool for defending yourself financially.

YOUR
NOTEBOOK

How to Talk with a
Reluctant Spouse

Convinced of the need to prepare for handling money, many women will get started immediately collecting the information needed for their notebooks, described later in this book. Sooner or later you will get to a part where you will have to ask your husband for some answers.

For some of you that will be no problem at all. You have an open and easy relationship with your spouse. He will be delighted to hear of your interest in financial matters and will encourage you in this project.

Some of you may find that your husband has assumed the role of your caretaker by default. He may enjoy giving up some of this burden, so don't assume he will object!

Others, when asking for help, will hit a brick wall, as these women did:

"I know I should know all these financial things, but he gets mad when I question him and leaves the room."

"He's so busy that the only time I have to ask him these things is on his day off or when he comes home tired late at night."

"It's not that he's trying to keep things from me; he just doesn't want to be bothered with it. And you can push them only so far. . . ."

If it seems reasonable that spouses should share financial information, then why don't they? Here are some answers I received from reluctant silent spouses:

Fear of Death

"That's too depressing. I don't want to talk about it."

Spendthrift Spouse

"If she knew how much we had, she'd spend every nickel of it."

Greed

"I want to have money, a lot of it, and I don't want my wife interfering."

Power

Money is the source of control and power. Some men enjoy forcing their wives to ask them for money. Very often these are men with great insecurity. When you ask them questions about money, you are threatening their power base. They have to take the control position because cooperating even the least little bit means complete loss of power in their eyes.

Enhancing Self-Image

Ridiculing or belittling the spouse may serve to shore up a fragile ego: "Tell her? You've got to be kidding. She'd just make a mess of things." If these remarks are true, then this is precisely the reason a head of household should begin preparing his spouse for life alone.

Hatred of Spouse

There are spouses who remain together who hate one another and would do nothing to benefit the other. They use money to hurt each other.

Embarrassment

Some men are embarrassed to let their spouses know they have lost money on investments or on business ventures.

Lack of Trust

"She'd tell everyone about our family business."

Lack of Concern

"Don't bother me; I've got a big sale pending [presentation to make, client in town, review coming up, a trial next week]." The wife's concerns are of little consequence in relation to the vastly more important life he leads.

Illegal Activity

Some spouses want no one, even their mates, to know where the money comes from.

Do you see your husband in any of these responses?

Some men who are reading this book may be saying, "You just don't understand. None of these men you have described are me. I would *like* to share with my wife, but when I try she shakes her head and says she doesn't want to hear about it."

So let's turn the question around. If it seems reasonable that women should want to know the family financial information, then why don't they? Here are some answers from women reluctant to hear.

Embarrassment

"I just don't know enough to discuss it." "I don't have a head for it." "I would make a fool of myself."

Fear of Responsibility

"I might create problems or make things worse."

Division of Labor

"I can't do everything. Taking care of four kids is all I can handle. It's more convenient for my husband to do the finances."

Tradition

"He has always taken care of that."

Do you see yourself in any of these responses?

In the first part of this book we looked at women whose stories showed us why financial information should be shared. Now we've established some reasons why spouses don't share financial information with one another. For those of you for whom the reasons to share win out, let's talk about how to persuade a reluctant spouse to talk.

For some, seeking professional counseling will be the answer. For others, the passage of time will help. After all, those four children *will* grow up! For those who want to begin now, start by having conversations with your husband *unrelated to money.*

Listen to yourself. Do you talk about a variety of topics? Or is it always about kids and crises? Are you argumentative, emotional, complaining, or confrontational? We may *think* we are having conversations when we really are not.

When you feel comfortable with your conversational skills, ask your husband your financial questions. The risk of upsetting the status quo may be all in your mind. Would upsetting the status quo be the great disaster you anticipate? Maybe not.

What if he doesn't respond to you? Back off and try again later.

Before you ask, you may feel more comfortable if you jot down your questions. Some men, accustomed to a fast-paced life, can't bear it if you don't get to the point.

Ask in a clear, nonaccusatory fashion.

Be confident!

Do all the work in the notebook you can do on your own first before you ask your husband for answers. Call your banker, broker, attorney, or insurance agent for missing pieces of information. Go through all the statements and information available to you first.

Show your husband the notebook when you ask for missing information. Use colored clips to mark the pages with missing information, so you don't have to be flipping through searching for something while your husband loses his patience.

Call it "**our**" notebook, not "my" notebook. Show him how your putting this information together is helpful to both of you. The fact that you are bringing information into the marriage could be very positive.

Recognize his past effort: "You've done such a good job of keeping track of our finances" or "You have things so organized that it was easy for me to put most of this together" or "You've done so well for us in our investments that I'd like you to help me learn more about what investments we have."

Focus on his strength. For example: "You've always been good at explaining things to me."

Show your faith in him: "I believe you can help me put this information together for our notebook very quickly."

Try to understand why he is reluctant to share.

Be specific in your requests. Ask "Would you tell me where last year's tax return is?" "Would you get me a copy of your benefits statement?"

Be present and future oriented. Don't criticize what he did or didn't do in the past.

Avoid labeling right and wrong.

Try not to be defensive.

Avoid absolutes like "You never" or "You always."

Work on one thing at a time. If you throw too many requests at him, he has the perfect opportunity to tell you that you are being unreasonable and walk away.

Set a time limit for this discussion. Don't drag it out.

Allow time for change.

What if your husband is always too busy or always too tired? Book a lunch date with him to get the answers you need. One woman told me that she and her husband go out to dinner to discuss *every* potentially volatile subject because they are both too well mannered to overreact in front of other people! Try talking while riding in the car when you have a captive audience. Try at informal times; taking a walk might work for the two of you.

What if he won't talk? If that happens, try asking him to write things down. Some spouses will be more comfortable with a request like "Would you mind jotting down the insurance policies you have in the safe at work?" or "Would you write on this page the names of our lawyer and our CPA?"

What if money is not the issue? Resistance to talking about money may be a cover for other hot spots in the marriage—like control, power, communication, or intimacy. If your husband won't talk or if the discussion quickly evolves into other issues, ask your husband to go to a marriage counselor with you to help come to grips with the underlying issues.

What if he won't cooperate and it seems as though it's never going to get any better? You've tried all these ideas and nothing works and your spouse refuses to go to a counselor with you. Then what do you do?

- You can always go to a counselor on your own to help resolve the issues within yourself. You will have to weigh the importance of accomplishing your goal to the success of the whole marriage.
- Force the issue. Get the information but threaten the status quo of the marriage.
- Go around him and obtain all the information you can from other sources. Settle for less than adequate information and less than adequate sharing in your marriage.
- Abandon your project. You don't *have to do anything about it*. You may choose to make peace with yourself for not accomplishing your goal, understanding that you will have a difficult time when your husband dies, divorces you, or becomes disabled. This, of course, is the least effective way of dealing with your finances and should be retreated to only as a last resort.

Now It's Time to Get to Work Compiling Your Notebook

Start today with day 1, step 1.

Do a little every day. Your notebook will be complete in thirty days.

You will have many answers to seek. Be persistent about getting them. If you let it slide, you'll never get around to it. Keep a list of the information you still need so that you won't lose track. Use colored paper clips to flag pages missing information. Obtain your facts in order, keep a list of what you need to ask your spouse, keep a list of information you need to seek elsewhere, and be diligent!

It will take time to assemble your notebook. You will learn a lot from this work. Everyone in your family will benefit, not just the surviving spouse. This notebook will be very helpful to your survivors when both spouses are deceased.

If you encounter resistance from others, remember that you are entitled to the information and have a right to ask for it. By doing this work, you are helping your family.

Your spouse may be protective of papers related to his business, stock options, group insurance, and so on. He may keep these papers in places where he can put his hands on them quickly. If so, don't remove them to your notebook. Make copies and replace the originals where he likes to keep them.

Day 1: Getting Organized

STEP 1.

Go shopping for these items:

1. Three-ring binder.
2. Three-hole punch.
3. Pack of three-hole-punched paper (unlined if you'll be using your computer and printer).
4. Sets of tabbed section dividers to give you at least twenty-two dividers.
5. Three-hole-punched plastic sheet protectors. Use these for items you don't want to punch holes in.
6. Colored paper clips.

STEP 2.

Label your dividers with these tabs:

Bank Accounts
Business Information
Contacts
Credit Cards
Debts Owed and Due
Disposition of Personal Property
Documents
Employment Records
Funeral Wishes
Insurance—Life
Insurance—Auto
Insurance—Homeowner's
Insurance—Other

Inventories
Investments
Personal Data
Real Estate
Retirement Plans
Safe-Deposit Box
Tax Return
Vehicles
Net Worth Statement

Day 2: Bank Accounts

STEP 1.

Punch three holes in a recent statement from each of the family bank accounts and file in the bank accounts section of your notebook. Certificates of deposit, checking, savings, and money-market accounts may have separate statements. Check for statements that may be mailed to addresses other than your home, such as to an office or a post office box. Don't assume the only accounts are the ones you know about—ask your spouse.

Once a year, replace these statements with more recent ones and remove statements from accounts that have been closed.

STEP 2.

Do you have too many accounts? Should you consolidate some of them?

STEP 3.

Clean out the catch-all drawers where you stick things like old bank statements. Have these accounts *really* been closed, or possibly are there assets still in them? To avoid confusion, if a bank account is truly closed, throw out old statements, passbooks, and checkbooks and cut up the ATM card. Keep checks you have written and check facsimiles for seven years, then discard.

Step 4.

Call your bank and confirm who has signature authority on your accounts other than the individuals in the account name. Make notes of this.

Day 3: Business Information

STEP 1.

In this section place copies of papers related to your/your husband's business interests, and business contacts and notes on what to do if you or your spouse can no longer run the day-to-day affairs of your business. Include instructions on the disposition of your business.

Day 4: Contacts

STEP 1.

Label a page in big letters across the top PERSONAL CON-TACTS.

STEP 2.

List your contacts—the people you may need to contact if your spouse dies, divorces you, or becomes disabled. Be sure to include your attorney, CPA, broker, banker, clergyman, business associates, physicians, and adult children. Even if you know these addresses and phone numbers from memory, write each person's role, name, address, and phone number, including area code. In times of stress your memory can play tricks on you. You will think of other personal contacts to be included in this list. Having all these names, address-es, and phone numbers in one place will be a blessing.

Day 5: Credit Cards

STEP 1.

Label a page CREDIT CARDS.

STEP 2.

Make four columns: KIND OF CARD, CARD NUMBER, IN WHOSE NAME, and ISSUER OF THE CARD.

STEP 3.

List *all* of your cards, including those with statements going to other addresses, such as your office address or a post office box. Don't assume the only cards are the ones you know about—ask your spouse.

List all department store charge cards.

STEP 4.

Complete the information for each card. The more cards you have, the easier it is to overspend. Should you cancel some of these cards to simplify your affairs?

Day 6: Debts Owed and Due

STEP 1.

Label the first page DEBTS OWED.

Set up seven columns: TO WHOM, AMOUNT, DEBTOR, %, PAYOFF DATE, PAYMENTS, and LOCATION OF PAPERS.

STEP 2.

In the first column list every person or institution to whom you owe money. Do not leave anything out. Include consumer loans, credit card debt, business loans, notes you have cosigned or guaranteed for others, money you have borrowed from friends or relatives, car loans, mortgages. Ask your spouse to look over the list; he may remember some you've forgotten. If something should happen to him, you do not want to be surprised by someone telling you that your spouse owed a large sum of money.

STEP 3.

In the second column list the amount owed.

In the third column list the debtor. This will be either you, your spouse, both of you jointly, or one of you jointly with another party.

In the fourth column note the interest rate.

In the fifth column write the payoff date.

In the sixth column note the frequency and size of payments, such as $800 monthly. Keep in mind that if you are paying the minimum payment on your credit card debt, you will never pay it off completely.

In the seventh column list the location of papers related to the debt. If your spouse dies, which of the debts you owed together will you keep in place? Which debts will you pay off? What assets will you liquidate to pay off the debt, or will you use insurance proceeds or cash reserves? You and your spouse will want to discuss this and make notes.

STEP 4.

When the debt is paid, line through the record and note the payoff date.

STEP 5.

Label the next page DEBTS RECEIVABLE.

Set up seven columns: DEBTOR, AMOUNT, OWNER, %, PAYOFF DATE, PAYMENTS, LOCATION OF PAPERS.

STEP 6.

In the first column list all persons who owe debts to you.

In the second column write the amount of the debt.

In the third column note to whom the money is owed—to you, to your spouse, to the two of you jointly, to one spouse and another party.

In the fourth column write the interest rate.

In the fifth column list the payoff date.

In the sixth column note the frequency and size of payments—for example, $200 monthly.

In the seventh column list the location of papers related to these debts. If your spouse dies, someone will need to contact those who owe him money regarding continuing the payments to his estate or paying off the debt.

STEP 7.

When the debt is paid, line through the record and note the payoff date.

Day 7: Disposition of Personal Property

STEP 1.

Label this page DISPOSITION OF PERSONAL PROPER-TY. You will need two pages, one for each spouse.

STEP 2.

Write these words: I WISH THAT THE FOLLOWING ITEMS OF MY PERSONAL PROPERTY BE GIVEN UPON MY DEATH TO THESE INDIVIDUALS, IF LIVING.

STEP 3.

Make two columns, PROPERTY ITEM and TO BE GIVEN TO.

STEP 4.

List items of personal property not included in your will and the person you want to receive each item.

STEP 5.

Sign and date this page.

STEP 6.

Your husband will repeat for his personal property and sign and date his page.

STEP 7.

If you change your mind, line through an old record and initial and date any changes you make. Better still, redo the entire sheet, sign and date the new sheet, and destroy the old one.

Families can spend a lot of time, money, personal energy, and anger over the disposition of the property of a deceased person. Why not spare your family this stress by taking care of this now? Although this is not a legal document, this list, *signed and dated,* can save a lot of wear and tear on your survivors.

Older people whose minds become unclear may give valuable items to caretakers, maids, yardmen, and others without being aware of what they are doing. Having this list can be all the argument your family will need for retrieving a family heirloom given away inappropriately.

You may have caretakers, maids, yardmen, friends, and others whom you want to have items of value to you and may think that your children would *never* remember these people without your specific legal instructions. If that is true, include those bequests in your will and tell your family or give them away now.

Tell your CPA or tax attorney about any gifts you make now over $10,000 in value. No, you cannot give one-half of an expensive Oriental rug this year and one-half next year without cutting the rug!

Day 8: Documents

Step 1.

Label this page DOCUMENTS. Set up two columns: DOCUMENT and LOCATION.

Step 2.

In column one list your important documents: wills, living wills, powers of attorney, organ gift donation papers, trusts, conservatorship requests, passports, birth certificates, marriage license, divorce decrees, deeds, car titles, military discharge papers, and any other important documents you can think of.

Step 3.

In column two note the location of each of these documents. If you like, use the plastic sheet protectors to file documents in this section.

Step 4.

Go to each location and check off if the document actually is there. If not, find it!

Step 5.

If you don't have updated wills, powers of attorney, and living wills, pick up the phone and make an appointment with your estate attorney.

This list can save you hours of stress when you are left alone. It can also save you money if you don't have to pay for document searches or don't have to pay to have these documents replaced.

Day 9: Employment Records

STEP 1.

Label this page EMPLOYMENT RECORDS FOR BENE-
FITS.

STEP 2.

The first section will be for Spouse A, so write one spouse's
name at the beginning of this section. Set up four columns:
DATES FROM TO, COMPANY, ADDRESS, and BENE-
FITS CONTACT.

STEP 3.

List all employment of permanent nature during which you
may have qualified for benefits, beginning with your current employment. If you know there is no benefit because
you weren't employed long enough to qualify or for other
reasons, don't list it.

STEP 4.

In the second section do the same for Spouse B.

This could be important for claiming retirement benefits,
life insurance proceeds, or health insurance coverage.

Day 10: Funeral Wishes

STEP 1.

You'll need two pages for this. Label each page FUNERAL WISHES FOR _____ , one for each spouse.

STEP 2.

Write the following on each page:

ORGAN DONOR CARD LOCATION _____
TREATMENT OF REMAINS _____
LOCATION OF PAPERS REGARDING COLUMBARIUM,
CEMETERY PLOT, OR MAUSOLEUM _____
MEMORIAL CONTRIBUTIONS SHOULD GO TO _____
AT THIS ADDRESS _____
PREFERRED LOCATION FOR MEMORIAL SERVICE _____
MUSIC/SCRIPTURE PREFERENCES _____
OTHER WISHES _____
NOTIFY THESE PEOPLE AT MY DEATH
     NAME   ADDRESS   PHONE

STEP 3.

Complete the page for each spouse. List as many names as you want at the last entry.

Although this has nothing to do with money, stress after the death of your spouse can be great. Why not make these decisions now?

Be sure to list all of the people who should be notified of a death. I have seen widows who, because of stress, have not been able to remember the last names of their husband's out-of-town friends and were not able to notify them. Because we lead complicated segmented lives, you and your spouse may not know the names, addresses, and phone numbers of all one another's friends.

Some will want to include instructions for the wake. I knew five people who left explicit instructions for joyous parties to celebrate their lives.

Day 11: Life Insurance

STEP 1.

Label this page LIFE INSURANCE.

Set up eight columns: COMPANY AND POLICY #, INSURED, BENEFICIARY, OWNER, FACE AMOUNT, PREMIUM DATE/AMOUNT, PHONE #, and LOCATION OF POLICY.

STEP 2.

List the data above describing each life insurance policy. You can find this information in the policy. Call the insurance company to confirm this data because it may have changed since you took out the policy. Be prepared with the descriptive data when you call the company. Also have the Social Security number and birthdates of the owner and the insured; they may be needed to open the gates to information. The insurance company may not talk with you about a policy unless you are the owner or the insured, so don't be angered if the company refuses to give you information on policies on your spouse that you do not own. For this information, ask the owner of the policy or the agent who sold you the policy to make the call.

If no 800 number is given on the policy, ask the company for it when you call their regular number and record it on this page of your notebook.

You may find the face amount has been reduced by loans or premium withdrawals. Because loans may be repaid in the future or may increase, note loans *in pencil* in the margin.

You may find that changes are needed in your family's life insurance coverage. Should beneficiaries be changed? Is the amount of insurance still appropriate? Should you and your spouse accept less coverage and stop paying premiums? If your children are already well provided for, should you name a charity as your beneficiary? If so, make a note to discuss these changes with your estate attorney.

You may find that one of you is *underinsured*. Many young parents make the mistake of underinsuring the mother/wife. If she were to die, money might be needed for child care, housekeepers, and taxis to replace her services until the children are grown.

Be sure to note the premium due date. If your husband were ill for an extended period, you would not want to miss the grace period allowed for paying the premium on his life insurance policy because you were too preoccupied to notice the due bill in the mail.

STEP 3.

You may discover old insurance policies that are no longer in force. Throw them away.

Day 12: Auto Insurance

STEP 1.

Label this page AUTO INSURANCE.

STEP 2.

List the agent, company, and phone number.

STEP 3.

Set up six columns: POLICY #, VEHICLE COV-
ERED, PREMIUM, DUE DATES, COVERAGE, and
DEDUCTIBLE.

STEP 4.

Fill in the columns, giving a brief description of the coverage, such as $100,000, $300,000, $25,000. These figures
represent the maximum the insurance company will pay to
other parties per person, per accident, and for property damage. The deductible is how much you must pay before the
insurance company will pay. File this page in the "INSUR-
ANCE—AUTO" section of your notebook.

STEP 5.

If vehicles are sold, line through the old record and add the
new record.

This exercise may cause you to rethink your coverage. Are
your deductibles too low? Higher deductibles might reduce

premiums significantly. Are you maintaining and insuring vehicles no longer needed by your family?

It is important to list premiums and due dates. If you are left alone, you would want to be prepared for these expenses.

Day 13: Homeowner's Insurance

Step 1.

Label this page HOMEOWNER'S INSURANCE. If you are renting, this would be RENTER'S INSURANCE.

Step 2.

As with auto insurance, list the agent, company, phone number.

Step 3.

Set up five columns: POLICY #, DEDUCTIBLE, COVER-AGE, PREMIUM, and DUE DATE.

Step 4.

Supply the information, including a brief description of the coverage. If there are separate policies on vacation homes, list them as such. File this page in the "INSURANCE—HOMEOWNER'S" section of your notebook.

If you read your homeowner's policy, you will discover some surprises. Is damage to a detached garage covered? Are items stolen from your car covered? Will your policy pay to repair a leaking roof or just to repair the damage caused by the leaking water?

Day 14: Other Insurance

STEP 1.

Label a page UMBRELLA POLICY.

STEP 2.

List the agent, company, phone number, policy number, premium, due date, and a brief description of the policy, including the deductible. File this page in the "INSUR-ANCE—OTHER" section of your notebook.

STEP 3.

If you have coverage on boats, RVs, jewelry, or any other items, label more pages appropriately and list information as above. File in the "INSURANCE—OTHER" section of your notebook.

STEP 4.

Continue adding pages for any other insurance coverage you may have, including professional liability coverage.

Day 15: Inventories

STEP 1.

In this section file inventories of precious metals, furnishings, jewelry, collections, art, guns, cameras, and other items of unusual value. Note location of papers, if applicable, and of photos of these items, if you have them.

STEP 2.

If applicable, list the names, addresses, and phone numbers of people to call for appraisals.

If your house is burglarized or if your estate attorney needs to place a value on your possessions, this information can be very helpful.

Day 16: Investments

STEP 1.

Assemble copies of recent statements from each of your brokerage accounts, mutual fund accounts, limited partnerships, bond holdings at banks, and trust investments. Punch holes in them and file in the "INVESTMENTS" section of your notebook. Once a year, change these statements.

Do you have too many brokerage accounts? Should you consolidate?

STEP 2.

If you keep your own stock and bond certificates, place in this section an inventory and indicate location of your certificates.

STEP 3.

If your statements or inventories don't show your dollar cost basis adjusted for stock splits and acquisition dates, make a note of this information for each asset. If you keep basis information elsewhere, note its location. If you keep this information on computer, give *step-by-step* instructions for accessing the information. File a current printout of your computer record in this section and update annually.

STEP 4.

If you or your spouse have employee stock options, file a copy of papers related to their exercise in this section of your notebook. Usually there are dates mentioned and dollar amounts at which they can be exercised. Some companies will allow a cashless exercise, in which an heir retains the right to exercise options if they have worth. The options may no longer be exercisable if your spouse has left the company. Check with the benefits manager of the company if you have questions.

Day 17: Personal Data

STEP 1.

Label a page PERSONAL DATA. Label the first section MEMBERS OF FAMILY. Set up four columns: LEGAL NAME, SOCIAL SECURITY #, DRIVER'S LICENSE #, and BIRTHDATE.

STEP 2.

Complete the columns for each spouse and for your children.

STEP 3.

Label the second section MARRIAGES AND DIVORCES. Note your marriages, your spouse's marriages, and your children's marriages, using the format "A married B on Date at Location." Note your divorces, your spouse's divorces, and your children's divorces, using the same format ("A divorced B on Date at Location").

STEP 4.

Label the third section PARENTS. Write THE PARENTS OF (spouse A) ARE: (names and addresses). THE PARENTS OF (spouse B) ARE: (names and addresses).

STEP 5.

Label the fourth section SIBLINGS and list their names and addresses, using the same format—THE SIBLINGS OF (spouse A) ARE: (names and addresses). THE SIBLINGS OF (spouse B) : (names and addresses).

While this may seem unnecessary, you never know when the need for this information will arise.

Day 18: Real Estate

STEP 1.

Label a page REAL ESTATE.

STEP 2.

List the address and legal description of each parcel of real estate you own by yourself or with others.

STEP 3.

Beside each entry copy the name of the owner *exactly* as it reads on the deed. In some states there is an important difference between "Joe and Jane, joint tenants," "Joe and Jane, joint tenants with right of survivorship," and, simply, "Joe and Jane."

STEP 4.

Note the location of each deed or file deeds in this section using plastic sheet protectors.

STEP 5.

If property ownership has changed, such as a joint tenant having died, contact your estate attorney. There is no good reason to put off clearing up these details. It will have to be done and better sooner than later, when you have been left alone.

STEP 6.

If a property is sold, line through the record and note the date of sale.

STEP 7.

For each property, give mortgage information—size of loan, interest rate, and payoff date.

Day 19: Retirement Plans

STEP 1.

In this section include a copy of a recent statement from each retirement plan you have. Include plans from current and previous employment, IRAs, 401(k)s, deferred compensation, and tax-deferred annuities. Change these statements once a year, discarding the old statements.

STEP 2.

Did the review of previous employment on day 9 bring to mind retirement plans from which you haven't heard in a while? Maybe they have lost track of you through address changes or computer glitches. Would it be worth a phone call to a prior employer?

STEP 3.

If you are still working, can you afford to retire? Given a few facts, a financial planner, insurance agent, CPA, or broker can help you answer that question.

STEP 4.

If you are already retired, at the rate you are spending, how long will your money last? A financial planner, broker, or CPA can help you answer that question.

STEP 5.

Make notes regarding what happens to your retirement benefit payments when you die and to your spouse's retirement benefit payments when he dies. Don't depend on what your spouse tells you or on what you remember. It could have been several years since you and he dealt with this. Look for it in writing among the benefit papers or call the company. Your circumstances may have changed since benefit choices were made. Are adjustments needed? Can adjustments be made?

Day 20: Safe-Deposit Box

STEP 1.

Label this page SAFE-DEPOSIT BOX.

STEP 2.

Write the number and bank branch location of your safe-deposit box. Write down in whose name the box is registered. *Don't guess*—ask the bank if you have no document (see page 106).

STEP 3.

Go to your box and make a list of the contents on this page in your notebook. It takes your key and a bank officer's key to get into the box.

STEP 4.

When you get home, in your notebook *write down where you put the key* to the deposit box.

Day 21: Tax Return

STEP 1.

In this section, file a photocopy of last year's tax return. Change once a year.

STEP 2.

On a separate sheet of paper, make two columns: YEAR and LOCATION OF TAX FILE.

STEP 3.

Start with last year. Write the year and the location of your records (receipts, canceled checks, etc.). For example, 1994—Attic. Every year add to your list the location of your tax file for that year, moving the old tax return to the tax file for that year.

Day 22: Vehicles

STEP 1.

Label this page VEHICLES.

STEP 2.

Set up four columns: MODEL/YEAR, STYLE/COLOR, OWNER, and LOCATION OF TITLE PAPERS.

STEP 3.

For each vehicle you own, list pertinent data. When a vehicle is sold, line through the record and note date of sale and to whom.

This may seem unnecessary to record, but if vehicles are stolen or there is a kidnapping or disappearance, having this information available quickly can be important. If you like, use the plastic sheet protectors to file title papers in this section, or make a copy of title papers and file in this section.

Day 23: Net Worth Statement

STEP 1.

In the section of your notebook tabbed NET WORTH STATEMENT, title the first page CASH AND EQUIVA-LENTS. Set up two columns: ASSET and OWNER. Further divide OWNER into four columns: HUSBAND, WIFE, JOINT, and TRUST.

STEP 2.

Under the ASSET column list all your checking and saving accounts. Refer to the "BANK ACCOUNTS" section of your notebook. Pencil in the current amount under the appropriate OWNER column. If the assets are owned as tenants in common, list one-half the value under HUS-BAND and one-half the value under WIFE.

STEP 3.

List all certificates of deposit. Pencil in the current amount under the appropriate OWNER column.

STEP 4.

List all money-market funds. Pencil in the current amount under the appropriate OWNER column.

STEP 5.

List all U.S. Treasury bills. Pencil in the current amount under the appropriate OWNER column.

STEP 6.

Total the amount of assets for each owner. Total the amount of cash and cash equivalents.

Day 24: Net Worth Statement

STEP 1.

Title the next page BONDS. Make two columns: ASSET and OWNER. Further divide OWNER into HUSBAND, WIFE, JOINT, and TRUST.

STEP 2.

Under the ASSET column list corporate bonds. Refer to the "INVESTMENTS" section of your notebook. Pencil in the current market value under the appropriate OWNER column.

STEP 3.

Repeat step 2 for the following assets: tax-free bonds, government and savings bonds, bond funds, and unit investment trusts (see page 121) composed of bonds.

STEP 4.

Total the amount of assets for each column. Total the amount of bonds.

Day 25: Net Worth Statement

STEP 1.

Title a page EQUITIES. Set up two columns: ASSET and OWNER. Further divide OWNER into columns for HUSBAND, WIFE, JOINT, and TRUST.

STEP 2.

Under the ASSET column write common stocks. Pencil in the current market value under the appropriate column. Refer to the "INVESTMENTS" section of your notebook.

STEP 3.

Repeat step 2 for preferred stocks, stock mutual funds, and unit investment trusts composed of stocks.

STEP 4.

Total the amount of assets in each column. Total the amount of equities.

STEP 5.

Title a page RETIREMENT ASSETS. Set up two columns: ASSET and OWNER. Further divide OWNER into columns for HUSBAND, WIFE, JOINT, and TRUST.

STEP 6.

Under the ASSET column, list annuities. Pencil in the current cash value under the appropriate OWNER column.

Refer to the "RETIREMENT PLANS" section of your notebook.

STEP 7.

Repeat step 6 for all your retirement assets—401(k), IRA, IRA rollover, profit-sharing plan, deferred compensation, SEP (see page 111), etc. If you will receive an income from your company after you retire and there is no current market value asset, do not list it here as part of your net worth.

STEP 8.

Total the assets under each column. Total the amount of retirement assets.

Day 26: Net Worth Statement

STEP 1.

Title a page REAL ESTATE. Set up two columns: ASSET and OWNER. Further divide OWNER into HUSBAND, WIFE, JOINT, and TRUST.

STEP 2.

Under the ASSET column list the real estate you own, beginning with your primary residence. Pencil in the market value under the appropriate OWNER column. Refer to the "REAL ESTATE" section of your notebook.

STEP 3.

Total the amount of assets under each OWNER column. Total the amount of real estate.

STEP 4.

Title a page BUSINESS INTERESTS. Set up two columns: ASSET and OWNER. Further divide the OWNER column into columns for HUSBAND, WIFE, JOINT, and TRUST.

STEP 5.

Under the ASSET column list the investment partnerships and business interests you own. Refer to the "BUSINESS INTERESTS" and the "INVESTMENTS" sections of your notebook.

STEP 6.

Total the amount under each column. Total the amount of business interests.

Day 27: Net Worth Statement

STEP 1.

Title a page DEBTS OWED <u>TO</u> YOU. Set up two columns: ASSET and OWNER. Further divide OWNER into four columns: HUSBAND, WIFE, JOINT, and TRUST.

STEP 2.

Under the ASSET column list your debtors. Pencil in the amount of the debt they owe under the appropriate OWNER column. Refer to the "DEBTS OWED AND DUE" section in your notebook.

STEP 3.

Total the amount of debt owed under each OWNER column. Total the amount of debt owed to you.

STEP 4.

Title a page OTHER ASSETS. Set up two columns: ASSET and OWNER. Further divide OWNER into four columns: HUSBAND, WIFE, JOINT, and TRUST.

STEP 5.

Under the ASSET column list personal property, antiques, precious metals, collections, art, or other items of unusual value that you feel should be a part of your net worth statement. Refer to the "INVENTORIES" section of your notebook.

STEP 6.

Total the amount of other assets under each OWNER column. Total the amount of other assets owned.

Day 28: Net Worth Statement

STEP 1.

Title this page LIABILITIES. Set up two columns: LIABIL-ITY and DEBTOR. Further divide DEBTOR into four columns: HUSBAND, WIFE, JOINT, and TRUST.

STEP 2.

Under the LIABILITY column list all the debts owed *by* you, including your mortgages, consumer loans, personal notes, credit card debt, margin debt, and debts you owe jointly with other parties. Refer to the "DEBTS OWED AND DUE" section of your notebook. Pencil in the amount under the appropriate DEBTOR column.

STEP 3.

Total the amount of liabilities under each DEBTOR column. Total the amount of liabilities.

Day 29: Net Worth Statement

STEP 1.

Title a page NET WORTH STATEMENT. Set up two columns: ASSET and OWNER. Further divide OWNER into four columns: HUSBAND, WIFE, JOINT, and TRUST.

STEP 2.

Under the ASSET column list cash, bonds, equities, retirement assets, real estate, business interests, debts owed to you, and other assets. Pencil in the totals from the preceding pages under the appropriate OWNER column.

STEP 3.

Total the amount of assets under each OWNER column.

STEP 4.

Underneath all of the assets in the first column, make a new header, LIABILITIES. Pencil in the totals from the preceding page under the appropriate column.

STEP 5.

Subtract the total liabilities from the total assets in each column.

STEP 6.

Add the subtotals from each OWNER column for your total net worth and write it at the end of this page. If either spouse has a net worth greater than $600,000 or if the total is over $1,200,000, make an appointment to discuss estate tax planning with your attorney. See page 143 for information about estate planning.

Day 30: Your Notebook

Congratulations! You have completed your notebook, an important tool for your financial self-defense. Now you have a financial record, in a form that you can use easily, that will be a valuable asset for you and for your family.

Share this notebook with your spouse. Be sure the people important to you know of its location. Keep this binder in an easy-to-retrieve spot, such as the home office or a highly visible bookshelf—*not* in the safe-deposit box!

Be sure to update your notebook and change the statements once a year. Some women choose year end, some choose a birthday or anniversary, some do it right after the taxes are filed.

Strategies for
Your Financial
Self-Defense

Dealing with the System

Inexperienced or indifferent employees, wrong forms, red tape, mistakes, and people who put you on hold and leave you there: all define "the system." Just remember it isn't you. *Many* smart, savvy people get the runaround and feel frustrated, helpless, and stupid.

When your husband is incapacitated or dies, you will be the one who deals with the insurance companies and the benefits department. Dealing with the system is frustrating for all of us at any time, but it can be especially taxing when you are under stress or when you've not had much experience. Here are some tips on learning to deal with the system.

- *Start now.* Learn skills of cutting through red tape and persuading people to be responsive to you. Don't always depend on your husband to handle the red tape for you.
- *Find a local contact.* Someone in a home office may be able to guide you through red tape.

- *Find a middle contact.* The last time I had a run-in with the system, the assistant of a regional manager said, "Why didn't you call me first? I could have gotten this done right the first time." Administrative assistants are often good folks to contact. Often they "run the show" while the boss is away playing golf.
- *Start at the top.* I like to start at the top and work my way down until I find someone who will help me. If you call the president's office, you will get his secretary or assistant. Start the conversation with, "I know you can help me. I need to _____ [apply for my deceased husband's pension, get a copy of the statement from ten years ago, etc.]." That person will refer you to someone below. When you get the next person say, "So-and-so in [name of president's] office said to call you. I know you can help me. I need to _____." If I actually got the president on my *first* call, to open my next call I would say, "[Name of president] said to call you. [Name of president] said you could help me. I need to _____." If you feel you don't have power, borrow someone else's!
- *Keep copies* of all the papers you send in to the system.
- *Write down the name and phone number of each person you talk to.* The next time you call you are sure to be asked, "Who told you that?" This tip deserves five stars for importance.
- *Write your request* in letter form before you call someone. Include all the essentials like names, account numbers, Social Security numbers, and so forth. Leave out nonessential details. People in the system don't want to hear about your life.
- *Send the letter* you wrote (see previous tip) if you don't get satisfaction from your phone call. Address the letter to a real person.
- *Smile,* even on the phone with someone. Use a pleasant voice.

- *Persevere.* Other people have gotten through this success-
  fully, and you will, too.
- *Ask other people to help you.* When your patience is wafer
  thin, call someone on your team of professional advisers.

Defending Yourself Financially before a Divorce

To avoid a financial disaster coinciding with a divorce, educate yourself: knowledge goes a long way. Become aware of your family assets and debts by drawing up a net worth statement *now*. Know what your family income is.

Be aware of your family spending patterns so you won't be broadsided by underestimating family expenses. Once child support and alimony are set, they are subject to modification only on proof of a material change in circumstances. Keep in mind that it costs both sides time and money to go back to court. So start reconciling your budget each month, as checking and charge card statements come in. Post expenses to budget categories by computer or by hand. A thrifty woman I know uses envelopes for receipts in various categories, so she includes her cash purchases as well. Then she totals each category on the outside of the envelope for the month. Some checking accounts and charge cards will post expenditures to budget categories for you.

Even though the title in which assets are held is not controlling, it is a good idea to have assets in your own name. If you have received an inheritance or gift, it is yours, *unless it has been used for family maintenance.* For example, a family farm in your name that generates a rental income that is reinvested in the farm is *not* a marital asset. A family home in your name used as your residence *is* a marital asset. Money you receive from your employment is a marital asset.

In some states a will written before a divorce is null and void with respect to a divorced spouse, so don't depend on it. However, a will written before a divorce is effective regarding distribution to children from that marriage, unless a new will is written.

If you expect a divorce in the future, should you clear out your joint accounts now? No. A judge will take this behavior of a marauding spouse into account. Are you worried that your spouse might clean out accounts, spend the money, and not be able to replace the assets when you divorce? If so, take care now to transfer some joint assets to your name and some to your spouse.

If you are worried about your livelihood should you divorce, understand that if the judge orders alimony or child support, your husband must pay this, even if he bankrupts. However, there are divorced husbands who fail to pay and divorced wives who are reluctant to garnish the husband's wages or enforce payment. If the judge orders a property settlement to you, it can be paid in a lump sum or in installments. If your divorced husband files bankruptcy, his obligation to pay a property settlement could be discharged. If possible, get your property settlement in full at the time of divorce.

If your spouse owns the house that you will live in as part of a divorce settlement, during the negotiations you should ask for a maintenance account. Note: This is not an interior decoration account.

Shelby White has written a thoroughly researched and very readable book, *What Every Woman Should Know about*

Her Husband's Money. Her in-depth discussion of the financial aspects of divorce will enlighten you.

Divorce is a changing area, and laws vary among states. It is best to consult a divorce attorney to be clear about how the laws can affect you.

How to Budget and How to Save

Several references have been made to keeping track of past and present family expenditures. It can seem so overwhelming that the temptation is great to guess at expenses, which can be dangerous. Here's how to start budgeting.

The computer method makes it easy in the long run. Visit your software dealer and see what he or she has to offer. Ask your computer-oriented friends what financial software they use. If you are recording by hand, ledger paper or a spiral notebook will suffice.

Collect the last six months of canceled checks, receipts, and credit card statements. If you don't keep these, start today and collect the next six months' worth. You will need your husband's help with his out-of-pocket expenses. Categorize your expenses: Charitable Gifts, Savings, Food, Eating Out (includes takeout and pizza delivery), Utilities and Cable, Household Maintenance (includes cleaning and yard services), Home Improvement and Repair, Clothing and Personal Care, Rent/Mortgage, Hobbies, Savings, Vacations,

Recreation, Business Expense, Education, Children's Allowance, Debt Repayment, Books and Magazines, Gifts, Automobile and Maintenance, Medical and Dental, Hobbies, and any other categories appropriate to you.

Figure your totals and percentages. You will be surprised at what you are spending in some of the categories. If you are trying to save money, decide how much and where you might trim. Then decide *how* you'll trim. Just saying "We'll eat out less" will not be helpful. Write down *specifically* what you and other family members will do to eat out less.

For the next three months post your expenses to categories. This will be easy since you already have everything set up. Since you are recording you may find yourself being more careful. Total your expenses and figure the percentages. How are you doing?

Setting aside a fixed amount of savings each pay period is one of the best ways to start or increase your saving. Other ways include the following:

- Contribute as much as you can to your 401(k) and other payroll deduction savings plans. What you don't see, you don't spend.
- Contribute the maximum to your IRA even if you don't get a current deduction.
- Give appreciated stocks in lieu of cash for your charitable gifts and put the difference in your out-of-pocket expense into savings.
- Pay off your highest-interest consumer loans before you try to start saving. The payments you are accustomed to making can then become payments into your savings.
- Encourage your teenage and college-age children to cover some of their expenses by having part-time jobs. For instance, some teenagers pay for their own car insurance and gasoline.
- Be a thrifty shopper; think before you buy; don't spend money you don't have.

- Cut back on expenses like personal care that can get out of hand easily. How much better is a $100 haircut than a $50 trim?
- Cut back on high-maintenance items like boats and vacation homes.
- Move to more affordable housing.
- Car pool.
- If you are not working, take a part-time job and save your paychecks.
- Use the public library.
- Use only one credit card.

Learning to budget for savings now is a great strategy for your financial self-defense, for two reasons: one, you will have savings later when you need them, and two, you will be accustomed to how the money is spent when you are left alone.

Remember, the goal of saving is to have a happy and abundant life. Don't neglect the occasional splurge, don't be pennywise and pound foolish, and don't make life miserable for yourself and your family.

Understanding Financial Accounts

Checking Accounts, Savings Accounts, Money-Market Funds

So that yours will not be among the one billion dollars in unclaimed assets, be aware of all your bank accounts, money-market funds, savings accounts, and CDs.

Banking rules vary from state to state. Where I live, if an account has joint tenants with right of survivorship in the title, and one tenant dies, the asset becomes the property of the survivor upon production of a certified death certificate, no matter what the deceased person's will says. If the checking account is in a single name, court papers are needed to gain access to the money. If money is needed from a single-name account to pay funeral expenses or bills, arrangements can be made with the local branch bank manager until court papers can be obtained. That is a good reason for visiting your local branch bank and making a point of knowing the people who work there and being sure they know you.

Some couples will prefer single-name accounts, giving one another signature power. Others prefer having two joint accounts, but think of them as "his" and "hers." While both joint tenants are still alive, either has access to all the money at any time, as does anyone with an authorized signature.

The banking world has changed dramatically in the last few years. Improvements in services have been made. Marketing enhancements have been added. Your advancing age may qualify you for more "perks." Because these features are there primarily to entice new money, don't expect your banker to call you and recommend you change to a less expensive or more value-added account. You are going to have to do that research yourself. Next time you are in the bank just ask for information on the kinds of accounts available.

The same is true for credit cards. When my credit card came up for renewal, I called the bank and asked them to cancel; I intended to switch to a credit card *without* an annual fee. When the phone attendant heard that, she volunteered to waive my annual fee if I continued to use their card. How many years have I paid that fee when it would have been waived if I had called earlier?

Deposit Boxes

At my bank, if a box is held in joint name, either party can have access, even after the death of a spouse. If a box is held in single name, no one without a power of attorney (other than the owner) can have access to that box. When the bank is informed of a death, the deposit box is sealed and cannot be reopened without letters of testamentary or letters of administration issued by the probate court. If the only copy of your will is in your safe-deposit box, a bank auditor, in the presence of a bank officer and a member of your family, can open the box to determine if the will is there and then close the box. Nothing can be removed without a court order. There is often no access to safe-deposit boxes on the weekend. When you rent a box (the cost is minimal), you are given a key. It takes your key and a bank officer's key to get into the box. You can see why it is best not to keep items that will be needed right after a death in the safe-deposit box.

Strategies for Getting Credit

All women over the age of nineteen should establish their own credit. Some women naively said, "I have a husband with a good job; I'll never need my own credit." It is often these women who find themselves alone and in need of a credit history. If you marry a second time, be sure the former spouse's name has been removed from all accounts. *Your* credit can be destroyed because of the debts run up by a first spouse.

How do you establish a credit history? First, call the merchants' credit association and ask to see your file. If you cannot find a listing, call the Chamber of Commerce—they will have the number. Even if you never had your own credit, you may have a file because all joint payments are reported in both names.

- Your branch bank officer may be able to help you get a credit card through the bank with a $1,000 limit.
- Use a credit card issued in joint name with your spouse if you cannot get your own. All payments to joint accounts are credited to both names.
- If you are given an authorized signature on your spouse's single-name credit card *when it is applied for,* then payments on that card should be reported in your name as well as in the name on the card.
- If you know the loan officer at your branch bank, keep a balance in your checking account and don't bounce any

checks. You may be able to take out a small personal loan. If you do, be sure to pay it back as soon as you can.

- You can borrow against your stocks and bonds in a margin account with a broker without having established a credit history.

Pension and Benefits

If your husband should die, would you know what benefits you would receive from his pension plan? Most wives have no idea what their husband's benefits are or what they will be should the spouse die. You may be in for a rude surprise—you may be getting nothing at all. It is worth a look at your husband's benefit statement or a call to the benefits department where he works. If you or your husband takes a new job, if possible keep copies of all the forms you complete. That way from the very beginning you'll know who benefits and how much.

Here are some tips for what you can do *now* to make handling benefits easier.

1. Many large companies offer seminars and outside speakers on benefits, investments, retirement, and insurance. If they are open to both employees and spouses (most are), then both of you should attend as many as you can.

2. Read the latest benefit statement. If your husband keeps forgetting to bring the statement home, call the human resource department for a copy. What if your spouse protests, saying he'll be fired or ridiculed if his wife calls his place of business? Don't believe him. To check this, I called ten businesses at random in the Birmingham, Alabama, area. Birmingham has as normal a business climate as other cities. All ten said no one would be ridiculed or be in danger of being fired. In fact, three of the businesses said this would be a "clerical nonevent." One said, "If everyone were

fired whose wife called in for a statement copy, no one would be left working here!"

3. Once you have the benefit statement in your hands, write down answers to these questions. That way you will learn to read the benefit statement more quickly.

- What lump sum benefit do I receive if my husband dies?
- What income will my husband receive if he becomes disabled?
- What is the definition of disabled? When does the income start? stop? Is it taxable?
- How much do we have in the company savings plan? How much do we contribute annually?
- How much do we have in the 401(k), profit-sharing, or money purchase plan? How much do we contribute annually?
- When my spouse retires, what is his projected benefit?
- If my spouse dies before he retires, what pension benefit would I receive?
- If my spouse dies after he retires, what pension benefit would I receive?
- Will my spouse receive deferred compensation?
- Does my spouse have stock options? What are the terms?

If you are working or have benefits from prior employment, repeat with your own benefit statement.

The answers will change as time passes. By writing them down, you'll discover things you never knew. Some things may need to be changed, like starting a payroll savings plan you couldn't afford before or changing an election on how retirement benefits will be received. You may want to alter the amount of disability income or change the names of beneficiaries.

You may be saying to yourself, I don't want to get these answers because it would be too hard, or, It would be too much trouble. How much harder will it be to get these answers if you are divorced or separated? Will you be more emotionally able to handle this now or when you are freshly widowed?

4. What if you and your spouse don't know the answers and can't read the statement? Make an appointment for the two of you with the benefits supervisor. One husband said to me, "I couldn't do that. They would look down on me if my wife and I came in for an appointment like that." When I passed that comment along to an employee benefits supervisor he said, "That's silly. I would think she was one sharp wife and that her husband was doing the right thing for her." If you can't go in, write a letter asking the questions, including a copy of the benefits statement. The employed spouse should sign it. Address it to a real person in the benefits department. Keep copies of both the letter and the statement. If you haven't heard from someone in twenty-one days, call and ask for a progress report. Remember that people who get attention are the people who ask for it.

5. If you are in a position to do so, encourage your employer to prepare videos on employee benefits that can be watched at home by both spouses. Encourage your employer to mail benefit statements home instead of giving them out at work.

6. Confirm your health coverage with the benefits department. If both you and your spouse work, you may discover you are paying for optional coverage from one employer that the other spouse can get for free. You may need to update benefit information if you find an oversight. For example, a woman filled out health insurance papers when she began working for a large corporation. After several months had passed she discovered that no health insurance premiums were being deducted from her paycheck. A quick

call to her benefits department revealed she had had no health insurance for eighteen months! Obviously she should have read her pay stub carefully each pay period, but how many of us are guilty of similar oversights? She did not leave work that day until she was fully covered.

Trust Accounts

A trust account holds assets that have been contributed by a donor and held separate for some reason for the benefit of someone. A trust document outlines how the trust assets can be invested, names a trustee and beneficiaries, and describes how income and principal will be distributed to those beneficiaries. With the exception of revocable living trusts, most trusts have separate tax numbers and require the filing of separate tax returns.

Children's Accounts

The Uniform Transfer to Minors Act (UTMA) allows accounts to be set up for minor children. An adult custodian is named—one custodian and one minor per account. Once gifts have been made to a child's account, they cannot be taken back. The child's unearned income over $1,300 is taxed at his parent's maximum bracket until he reaches the age of fourteen. Then his income is taxed at his own bracket. When he reaches the age of majority, the assets belong to him. He can present proof of ownership and age to claim the assets in his own name.

Retirement Plans

There are different kinds of retirement plans. If you or your husband work for a company that agrees to pay you a specific amount when you retire, then you have a defined benefit pension plan. These are losing their popularity and are being replaced by defined contribution plans. In a defined contribution plan the dollars that are put in are specified, not the dollars of benefit to be taken out.

Profit-Sharing Plan

One type of defined contribution plan is profit-sharing. Your company, if it wishes, can make its contributions to the plan contingent on making a profit. A plan may allow the employer to skip a year of payments. The maximum annual contribution is 15 percent of earned income or $22,500, whichever is less.

Money Purchase Plan

A money purchase plan is a defined contribution plan that allows up to 25 percent contribution or $30,000, whichever is less. The employer cannot skip a year of contributing, even if the company doesn't make a profit. If you are covered by more than one type of defined contribution plan at work, the total contribution to all plans cannot exceed $30,000. However, if you have a second job, you can have up to an additional $30,000 contribution for that second source of income.

Simplified Employee Pension Plan

Another type of defined contribution plan is a SEP, a simplified employee pension plan. This plan is popular with self-employed individuals and with small companies. The government paperwork is not as much as with a full-blown profit-sharing plan, money purchase plan, or 401(k). The maximum contribution is 15 percent of earned income or $22,500, whichever is less.

401(k)

A 401(k) is a hybrid profit-sharing plan. The employee contributes part of his gross pay before taxes are taken out. This

year (1996) the maximum contribution to
$9,500 (changes annually). Sometimes the c
match your contribution, so this is just like
raise. Since your contributions are pretax, the more ...
you put in, the less money you show as earned and the less
current taxes you pay. There are usually four or more investment choices from which a participant may choose in the
401(k), usually a bond fund, a stock fund, a balanced fund,
and a safe harbor (fixed-rate or money-market fund).

IRA

An IRA is an individual retirement account. As of this writing, working people can each contribute $2,000 a year and
a worker with a nonworking spouse can contribute a total of
$2,250 to the couple's two IRAs. If you and your spouse are
not covered by a retirement plan, then the contribution is
fully deductible. If one of you is covered by a retirement
plan where you work, the IRA contribution for either of you
may not be fully deductible.

The money in retirement plans grows tax-deferred.
When they are withdrawn, the investment earnings and
untaxed contributions are taxed as ordinary income.

IRA Rollover

If you retire or leave your company, you may be able to roll
over the assets in your plan to an IRA rollover. Many plans
will have up to a five-year vesting schedule, meaning you are
entitled to only a portion of the employer contribution during the first five years of your employment. The money an
employee contributes to a 401(k) is always vested. When you
roll over the money in your retirement plan, it is paid directly to your new custodian, the institution that holds your
IRA. You can invest your rollover funds in a variety of ways.
You can combine your IRA rollover distribution from an old
plan with your normal $2,000-a-year IRA, thus cutting
down costs and the number of statements you receive. You

also create a larger pool of investment capital, which may open up more opportunities for you. If you leave the IRA rollover separate, you can "roll over the rollover" into a new retirement plan at a new place of employment in the future, if your new plan allows it. If you have combined the rollover with a $2,000 annual IRA, you lose that portability.

If withdrawals from all of the tax-deferred accounts just mentioned—profit-sharing, 401(k), pension, IRA—are made before age 59 1/2, there will be an IRA surcharge of 10 percent, in addition to taxes on the amount withdrawn.

Tax-Deferred Annuities

Another kind of tax-deferred investment is an annuity. During the growth period the earnings are tax-deferred. You are taxed when you make withdrawals. A fixed annuity provides a guaranteed competitive rate of return and the principal. A variable annuity does not have a guaranteed return; instead it features investment in subaccounts similar to mutual funds designed to give the investor potential to generate greater return on capital.

In the variable annuity contract, the insurance company promises, among other things, to keep the portfolios in a segregated account, so those funds may not be used to pay the company's obligations. Most variable annuities guarantee to provide an estate equal to your investment, less withdrawals, at the time of your death.

Nearly every variable annuity offers many types of investment portfolios (for example, domestic and global growth, income, money-market funds). You could put money in one, several, or all of the portfolios within a particular annuity. If your investment goals or market conditions change once you've allocated your investment, variable annuities give you the flexibility to move from one type of portfolio to another, usually without charge and always without taxation.

Like a mutual fund, variable annuities are professionally managed. These investments may fluctuate in value. At times your account may be worth more or less than you put in. If you have to withdraw money when your account is down, you could suffer losses.

Unlike fixed annuities, nearly all variable contracts have management fees and administrative charges that are assessed either as a flat fee or a percentage of your account value.

Most fixed and variable annuity contracts impose charges for early withdrawal. Typically the charges are higher in early years, then diminish to zero. Moreover the IRS imposes a 10 percent tax penalty on earnings withdrawn before age 59 1/2, as with an IRA or 401(k) plan.

Understanding Investments

The best thing you can do to defend yourself where investments are concerned is to understand what you have. Start with learning to read your brokerage statement. If your broker hosts an annual statement reading clinic, attend it. Don't be afraid to ask questions. If you like, make an appointment with your broker to review your statement after market hours. Since brokers have copies of monthly statements, you can review together over the phone after market hours, although face-to-face meetings are better.

Cash Investments

Cash investments include money-market funds (taxable, tax-free, or government), U.S. Treasury bills, and certificates of deposit (CDs). *Money-market funds* earn interest daily and are priced at a constant $1.00 per share. The interest rate changes daily and is low, relative to long-term bonds. *U.S. Treasury bills* mature in three, six, nine, or twelve months.

The minimum investment is $10,000. They are bought at a discount (less than face value) and mature at par (face value). The yield is fixed when the bill is bought and is similar to yield on money-market funds. Market price of the bill can fluctuate, although variation is minimal because of the short time to maturity. *Certificates of deposit* represent sums of money placed with a bank earning a guaranteed interest rate for a stated length of time. The interest is normally paid semiannually.

Common Stocks

Stocks are shares of ownership (equity) in companies. Some stocks pay dividends quarterly. If you care about current income, you'll want to know about the dividends your stock pays, that is, the dollar amount, the percentage compared to what you paid for the stock, how secure the dividends are, and how often they have been increased in the past. Although healthy dividends are an attractive feature, most stocks are bought for their growth potential. The stock price is controlled by supply and demand. Many factors influence people to buy or sell, thus driving the price. One factor is earnings. Another is earnings potential, or the company's profit or potential to make a profit. A company that consistently increases its profits from increased sales is called a growth company. Normal growth companies are expected to show an 8 percent to 12 percent growth in profit annually. Aggressive growth companies are expected to show around a 20 percent growth in profit from one year to the next. To find out what the profits are for the last ten years, look in *Standard & Poor's Stock Reports* or in *Value Line Investment Survey*. Both of these can be found in the reference section of your library. Your broker should have these references. Your broker will also have the *Standard & Poor's Monthly Stock Guide,* where earnings per share are reported for the last five years.

Some companies are riskier than others because of their size, the nature of their business, or the level of debt they carry. Standard & Poor's gives a safety rating to companies that is a general indicator of the level of their risk. You can also read the *Value Line* or *Standard & Poor's* reports of the ratio of debt of the company to its total capitalization. Capitalization is long-term borrowing and investment by owners. An average debt load is about 30 percent debt to total capital. Some industries have higher debt than others, so it's best to compare the debt level of a company to that of other companies in its industry group, rather than to stocks in general. For instance, utilities have a higher debt level than food companies. If you want to compare a stock to others in its industry group, ask your broker for his or her research department's statistical summary. Or look in *Value Line*, where stocks are reported by industry group.

You may have heard the term *P/E,* or *price to earnings ratio,* when stocks are discussed. That means price divided by earnings (profits). Take the price of a stock—let's say $20 per share—and divide it by the earnings (profits) per share—let's say $2: there you have the P/E of 10 in our example. If two companies make can openers and one of those companies sells at a P/E of 27 and one at a P/E of 9, you might assume that the P/E of 9 represented a better value per dollar of investment. That may be true and bears investigating. You may find that the P/E 27 company has just developed a new technology or has opened new markets and expects its earning to escalate more quickly than the P/E 9 company. The P/E 9 company may have lost big customers or talented management or may have a poor-quality balance sheet. That's why it is more meaningful to compare the P/E of a stock to others *in its industry group* than to the P/E of the stock market as a whole or to the P/E of a stock in another industry group.

Stock Analysis

Stocks are subject to two forms of analysis—technical and fundamental. Technical analysis answers the question "What are the numbers?" and fundamental analysis answers the question "What is the story?" Technical analysts look at charts and graphs of price and don't care what the company actually does. Fundamental analysts ask questions like "What is the company doing to increase market share or to lower production costs? What new products are being developed? How are the people in management positions compensated? What is the company's competition?" Technical analysis tells you *when* to buy or sell. Fundamental analysis tells you *what* to buy or sell. You can obtain technical and fundamental analysis free of charge from your broker. If you want to obtain information on your own, consult the ads in financial periodicals for services and newsletters that will provide stock analysis to you for a subscription fee.

Trading Practices

Stocks trade on the exchanges or on the over-the-counter market (NASDAQ). The New York and the American are the two largest stock exchanges. If you go to New York, visit one of the exchanges for an exciting, fun, and educational morning. The over-the-counter market is a computer network of traders who make markets in stocks of companies not traded on the exchanges. Stock is usually traded in round lots of one hundred shares, although you may buy in any amount. You may place a market order, meaning the best price at the time the order gets to the floor of the exchange, or a limit order, in which you specify the price at which you are willing to buy or to sell.

Preferred Stocks

A preferred stock is special because its holders receive their dividends before common shareholders and are paid before common shareholders in the event there is a liquidation of the company. Usually preferred dividends are higher than common dividends but do not increase; common dividends can be increased. Cumulative preferred means that missed dividends accumulate to be paid later. Preferred shareholders do not vote at the annual meeting; common shareholders do. A convertible preferred can be exchanged for a certain number of common shares.

Bonds

Bonds represent funds that have been loaned to companies or to governments at a specified interest rate and a specified maturity date when the principal will be repaid to the bondholder. Interest is usually paid twice a year.

If bonds are insured or if they are escrowed to maturity (money earmarked to pay them off), they receive a Standard & Poor's rating of AAA. Issuers of bonds that have a good record of paying principal and interest and who have solid sources of revenue are given a Standard & Poor's rating of AA. Together with the next two ratings, A and BBB, these make up the category called investment-grade bonds. Anything rated below that is called junk by some and high yield by others.

Corporate and government bonds are most often traded in blocks of $1,000. Tax-free bonds are usually traded in blocks of $5,000 face value. Bondholders come ahead of stockholders should there be a liquidation of the company. Bond prices fluctuate depending on what interest rates are doing. Theoretically, when interest rates go up, bond prices go down; when interest rates go down, bond prices go up. If you bought the bonds with the idea of selling them before the maturity or if you bought junk bonds, you'll need to watch the market price.

Zero Coupon Bonds

Some bonds are called zero coupon, meaning they pay no interest. They are bought at a discount to face value and mature at par (face value). If they are tax-free municipal bonds, this is generally an income tax–free event. If they are taxable bonds, you must pay tax every year *as if* interest had been received. Because of this, you rarely see taxable zero coupons in taxpayer accounts; usually taxable zeros are purchased in a retirement account where tax is not paid. Zero coupon bonds are often bought with maturities coinciding with significant events, such as college years or retirement dates. The theoretical value of zero coupon bonds accrues in a stair-step fashion from the purchase date to the maturity date *as if* interest had been received and reinvested back into the bond. When you buy a zero coupon bond, you are told what internal interest rate is assumed. The *market price* of zero coupon bonds will actually fall somewhere to the right or left of a bond's theoretical value line, as interest rates fluctuate.

Taxable Equivalents of Tax-Free Bonds

INCOME TAX RATES FOR 1996, MARRIED FILING JOINTLY

Income	*Payment to IRS*
$0–$39,000	15%
$39,001–$94,250	28%
$94,251–$143,600	31%
$143,601–$256,500	36%
Over $256,500	39.6%

How can you tell the taxable equivalent of a tax-free bond? First, figure how much you pay in taxes. If you pay 31 percent marginal tax bracket to the federal government (see chart) and 5 percent to your state, your total income tax is 36 percent. You get to keep 64 percent of every additional dollar you make. Next, divide the interest rate of the tax-free bond by 1 minus your tax rate. In the example, 1 minus .36 (combined state and federal tax bracket) equals .64. If a tax-free bond yields 5 percent, divide 5 by .64. The taxable equivalent is 7.8 percent. At the 36 percent tax bracket, a 5 percent tax-free bond would be a better choice than a 7 percent taxable bond, all other things being equal.

Use this formula to compare the yields on taxable and tax-free bonds.

Here is the formula:

$$\frac{\text{tax free yield}}{1 - \text{tax rate}} = \text{taxable equivalent}$$

Tax-Free Bonds

Interest earned from bonds issued by states, municipalities, and state agencies are generally free from federal income tax and also free of state income tax to residents of the issuing state. For instance, as an Alabama resident, if I buy a state of Georgia bond, I pay no federal tax, but I do pay state income tax on my interest. My Alabama bonds, however, are federal and state tax–free. Puerto Rican bonds are income tax–free to residents of *all* states.

Tax-free bonds are issued as book entry or registered. Book entry means a custodian (bank or broker) "holds" your bond and receives interest electronically into your account in your behalf. Registered means the interest payment is sent to the registered bondholder, whether custodian or individual investor. Book entry is a much less expensive process, and that is the way most bonds are issued today. Several years ago bonds were issued as "bearer" bonds. The bearer, or bondholder, clipped a coupon from the paper-printed bond and redeemed it for tax-free interest. This cumbersome, expensive, and risky process has been discontinued for new bonds, but there are still a few old "bearer" bonds around.

Riding the Yield Curve

If you plot a graph with the vertical axis the percentage rate of bond yields and the horizontal axis bond maturity, you will see a line called the yield curve. Ride the yield curve; this means look for the elbow of the curve before interest rates begin to flatten and buy your bonds in those maturities. Today that is around eight to ten years. See the plot in the accompanying graph. It is unnecessary to invest for longer periods with very little increase in yield unless you are planning for later maturity dates to coincide with events like weddings, college, or retirement. Longer-term bonds have greater market fluctuation than shorter-term bonds.

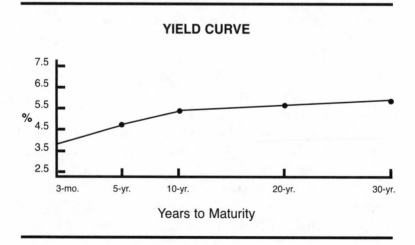

YIELD CURVE

Years to Maturity

Mutual Funds

Open-End Funds

Mutual funds have grown in popularity with investors. They are portfolios of stocks or bonds managed by professionals. When you buy or sell a share of a mutual fund you buy or sell an undivided interest in the underlying basket of securities. Everyone who sells shares of an open-end mutual fund on the same day sells at the same price. The price is figured at the close of the trading day and is based on the value of the investments in the basket at the market close. This is to "mark the market," and the resulting price is called the net asset value.

The price paid to buy shares of an open-end mutual fund can be the net asset value, in the case of no-load funds, or an asked price including a sales commission in the case of front-end load funds. Back-end load fund shares have no sales charge when bought but do charge a commission to sell during the first few years the shares are held. Front-end load sales charges are reduced by volume discounts.

Open-end mutual funds pay the shareholder cash when he redeems his shares. If there is not enough cash on hand to redeem shares, the mutual fund managers are forced to sell securities. When investors buy shares, the cash they pay goes into the fund. The managers of the fund must invest this cash. This influx and demand for cash may come at inopportune times for investments to be bought or sold, so managers may be forced into untimely buys or sells.

Mutual fund shareholders are taxed on the net capital gains taken all during the year, even when they did not own the mutual fund shares. Mutual fund shareholders receive a taxable net capital gain distribution once a year. Distributions of income from mutual funds can be distributed as often as monthly.

Closed-End Funds

Closed-end fund shares are not redeemed or sold by the fund itself. Their shares are bought and sold on the New York Stock Exchange just like shares of stock. If you want to redeem your shares, you simply sell them to someone else. The investments in the fund remain intact, resulting theoretically in a more well-managed fund. Closed-end fund shares can fluctuate in price all day long, just like shares of stock. They can trade at a discount or at a premium to their net asset value. A normal brokerage commission is charged to buy or sell closed-end fund shares on the exchange.

Global Investing

Investments in other countries are becoming more popular. To make the purchase of foreign shares easier, stocks trade in dollar-denominated American Depository Receipts (ADRs). Mutual funds focusing on specific countries are available for trading, as are global funds.

Initial Public Offering

When companies go public, an initial public offer (IPO) of the stock is made. Everyone buys at the same price and no brokerage commission is charged to the new shareholders.

Asset Allocation

An investor decides how to allocate his portfolio among stocks, bonds, and cash. The more safety conscious you are, the more *cash* investments you will have. The more interested in growth you are, the more *stock* investments you will have. Because of the promise to pay interest and principal, *bonds* are considered less risky than stocks. But keep in mind that bonds can fluctuate in market price. No one investment satisfies all three needs of safety, income, and growth. It is not a good idea to have all your money invested in *one* security; diversity is important to preserve your capital.

Private Money Managers

Some investors hire private money managers to manage their portfolios of investments. Generally you must have at least $100,000 to qualify for this kind of service. You will have a portfolio of identifiable securities. You give your money manager authority to trade these securities on your behalf without consulting you prior to trading. You pay a management fee to the manager and brokerage fees to your broker. Some brokerage houses combine these two into a wrap fee at a percentage of the market value of the securities. This can save you money if your manager trades frequently or has several small positions. A wrap fee can cost more than fee plus commission if there is little turnover in your portfolio and if you have fewer, larger positions. Money managers have a theme or style to which they adhere, such as value, small cap, or aggressive growth. Since not all styles of investing are successful at all times, you want to be diverse and have more than one style in your portfolio. An investor with less than $200,000 can use mutual funds until the capital has grown enough to hire more than one manager. One of the advantages of using a private money manager is that you are taxed only on the transactions in your personal portfolio. See discussion under mutual funds.

Annual Review

You should have a review with your broker at least once a year. During this time you will update your broker on changes in your family or financial situation. You should review the performance of your money managers and your investments to determine if they are still meeting your goals. That means that when you started investing you set goals. If you didn't, try writing them down now. Most of us have some idea of what we want from our investment portfolios. It will be much easier to evaluate performance and to make investment choices if you've written down your goals.

Learning More about Investing

Two books for learning more about investing, both by Peter Lynch, are *One Up on Wall Street* and a sequel, *Beating the Street*. Also, your broker will be able to provide brochures on a variety of investment topics. On most television cable systems there is a channel that gives financial information all day long. Financial publications such as *The Wall Street Journal* and *Value Line* and all the financial magazines offer trial subscriptions. Why not try one or two?

Understanding Insurance

Why aren't women as likely to have insurance coverage as men? Because common perception is that their lives have less economic value. There are three groups of women for whom it is crucial to have substantial coverage: women who are significant income sources for their families (and themselves), women whose services as mothers and homemakers would cost a good deal to replace, and women who are key figures in their businesses.

Types of Insurance

Survivor Coverage

Survivor coverage is the amount left to the insured's surviving dependents. How much survivor coverage should you have? First be aware of all debts. Decide with your spouse which of these debts should be paid if he died. Should assets be sold to pay these debts? If so, which assets? Since a public market exists for stocks and bonds they can be sold with ease. There is no public market for businesses or for real estate. If there is no public market, who should buy the assets in question? If there are insufficient assets to cover debts but you still have enough money to live on, use insurance. You don't have to pay off debts, but you should have the ability to do so. Next, determine what your living expenses would be if the insured were to die. Then determine what sources of family income will continue or start after your spouse's death. Will you be working? Include your own income and the insured's pension benefit if it is to be paid to the survivor. Make up the difference with insurance. Third, if there are college educations to pay for, what side funds have been created to cover them? If you do not have assets to cover college tuition costs, add that estimate to the amount of insurance needed. Count on $10,000–$25,000 per year. Finally, add extraordinary expenses like weddings, cars, and major home repairs if you do not have assets to cover these. This should give you an idea of the amount of coverage you need.

Disability Coverage
A living death from disability can be worse on the survivor than a death itself. This is the most important type of insurance you will have, and it is the most often overlooked. Go through the same exercise as above to determine the amount of coverage needed should either spouse become disabled.

Long-Term Care
If you are over sixty and in reasonably good health, look into long-term health care coverage. The chances are great that one or both spouses will need long-term nursing care for at least two and one-half years. The average cost of nursing home care in the United States is $100 per day, or $36,000 a year. For a fraction of what it would cost, you can insure most of your long-term care for life.

Health Care

If you or your spouse is working, you may be covered by a group health insurance plan. If not, look for other group plans for which you may qualify, such as one through a professional association. Failing that, shop around for the best coverage you can find for the premium you can afford. If you are covered by Medicare, you probably know that Medicare supplements are available as A (basic) to J (comprehensive). Write down all your health care policy numbers, insurance companies, and names of insured. You may have bought several supplements to Medicare; you need only one. Ask your life insurance agent to read through your Medicare supplement policies with you and help you choose one. Be sure to file claims and *use* your policy if the need arises.

Wealth Replacement

Both you and your spouse can each pass $600,000 of single-name assets to your heirs free of estate taxes. Therefore, if you have titled your assets so each of you owns up to $600,000, you can pass a total of $1,200,000 free of estate taxes. If you and your spouse have a joint estate in *excess* of $1,200,000, estate taxes must be paid when the second spouse dies, thus reducing the size of the estate you pass on to your heirs. *By acting now while both of you are still alive, you can insure that your heirs will have this wealth replaced.* Your heirs can own insurance on you and your spouse outside your estate in the amount that you estimate will be paid in estate taxes. The proceeds of this policy will be paid outside your estate *tax-free* without increasing the size of your estate. A joint policy on you and your spouse, taken out while both of you are alive, will be less expensive than insuring both of your lives separately. Circumstances may dictate that you have a wealth replacement trust that owns the insurance rather than your heirs owning the insurance directly. Your estate attorney can advise you on this matter.

Common Insurance Terms

Here are some common insurance terms you may encounter as you read your policies:

Term Insurance

A person's life is insured temporarily for a guaranteed benefit over a specified amount of time. Actuaries can figure how many people in a category will die within a certain time. As the frequency of deaths increases with age, so do term life premiums. Term insurance is used when there is a temporary problem to solve, such as increasing coverage on your life while your children are small.

Group Term

The lives of a large group of people, such as an association or a group of employees, are taken together to offer coverage to all without medical examination.

Level Term

Insurance companies take increasing annual premiums and average them together for five-, ten-, fifteen-, or twenty-year-level premiums. If you keep the policy in place for the entire period, this is less expensive than annual renewable term.

Whole Life

The premium is guaranteed never to go up and coverage is guaranteed never to go down over your whole life. With whole life you have a guaranteed premium and guaranteed death benefit—the insurance company assumes the risks.

Interest-Sensitive Whole Life

Both the premium and the face value are guaranteed, although the interest rate is not. If the interest rate earned goes higher, then the overage not needed to pay the cost of the coverage can be used to increase the death benefit, increase the cash value, or "vanish" the premium. If the interest rate goes down, then it will take a longer period of paying in premiums and earning interest to "vanish" the premium.

Universal Life

Every piece is a moving part. Neither the death benefit, the premium, nor the interest rate is guaranteed. Option one targets a level death benefit while option two increases the death benefit. If interest rates are high and the premium is low, enough money will be earned by the policy to vanish the premium in a few years at a given death benefit. If interest rates go down and premiums remain the same, the premium will have to be paid for a longer period of time and you may have to pay more annual premium to maintain a level death rate. If interest rates go down and if you want to stop paying premiums, you may have to accept a lower fixed face amount of death benefit. Premiums are flexible (can be skipped).

Variable Life

Instead of earning interest at a stated rate, cash value can be invested in a choice of professionally managed accounts similar to mutual funds. Death benefit can be guaranteed. If investment choices are successful, cash value can grow faster than in a fixed-rate policy. You can lose cash value if investment choices are not successful; therefore variable policies are often chosen by young people who have high risk tolerance. This type of policy would be chosen when the potential of generating a large cash value is important. Premiums are flexible (can be skipped).

Vanish

To "vanish" a policy premium, you must pay enough into the policy in the early years to maintain it without having to pay additional premiums in the later years.

Cash Value
The amount of money accumulated within a life insurance policy not needed to pay charges and expenses. Another term for this is *accumulated value*.

Surrender Value
The cash value less surrender charges. Surrender charges disappear after twelve to twenty years.

1035-exchange
A tax-free exchange of the assets in one policy to a new policy with the same owner, insured, and beneficiary. After the exchange, the owner can change the beneficiary if desired.

Mutual Company
Owned by the policy holders.

Stock Company
Owned by the stockholders.

Dividends
If fewer people die than expected, if interest yield is high, or if costs are kept down, mutual companies return premium dollars not needed to the owner of the permanent (not term) policy and call it a dividend. This is a partial return of premium, not a true dividend. These dividends can be taken as cash, used to reduce the premium, left on deposit at interest, utilized to purchase paid-up additional life insurance, or used to purchase term insurance to increase the death benefit.

Premium
The cost paid to put a policy in place consisting of mortality risk charge, expenses, and commissions. If you keep paying premiums into a policy, eventually you will accumulate enough money in the policy to force the death benefit to increase. There are hybrids that combine term and whole

life to keep premiums low and still have a guaranteed face amount.

Beneficiary

The person who gets the money when the insured dies, income tax–free, is the beneficiary.

Owner

The person or entity that owns the policy. If the owner is also the insured, when the owner dies the proceeds of the policy are included in his gross estate for estate tax purposes, even though the proceeds are paid to someone outside the estate. Naming a beneficiary other than your estate does not take the proceeds out of your estate. The only way to not include the proceeds in the insured's estate for tax purposes is for the owner to be someone other than the insured. Sometimes adult children or insurance trusts own insurance outside the insured's estate. Ownership is important.

Endowed Policy

A policy into which enough premiums have been paid to cause the cash value to equal the death benefit.

Supplemental Retirement Income

Although the primary purpose of insurance is to insure your life for the benefit of others, many people see the return of premium and loans against cash value as a tax-free supplement to their retirement income. These withdrawals reduce your coverage, of course. When you die and the policy pays your beneficiary, any loan against your cash value is repaid out of the death proceeds and the beneficiary gets the remainder. There will be a point at which you must stop withdrawing dollars or else the policy will collapse.

Corridor

The difference between the net cash value (after debit is subtracted from your cash value) and the face amount. If the specified corridor is not present, then the withdrawals you make are considered taxable withdrawals of earnings, not tax-free borrowing against cash value. There must be a corridor in order for the contract to remain a life insurance policy. If the corridor is not present, the contract becomes an annuity and future withdrawals will be taxable on earnings, last in, first out.

Safety Ratings

When you purchase a policy, be sure to inquire about the company's safety as measured by A. M. Best, Moody's, Standard & Poor's, and Duff and Phelps relative to other companies.

Life Insurance Trust

When you want insurance on your life owned outside your estate, your attorney can draw up a life insurance trust. The premiums are paid by the trustee, perhaps with gifts of money from you. A responsible adult child is often named the trustee. Trusts are useful if you have spendthrift children, problems with sons- or daughters-in-law, potential divorces among your offspring, grandchildren from multiple marriages, or other family complications that would rule out your children owning a policy on you directly. Talk to your estate attorney about a life insurance trust if you think it might be of value to you.

A Few Things to Know about
Homeowner's Insurance

The coverage you have to replace your home is calculated by
a computer based on factors like square footage, presence of
decks, a basement, a fireplace, and so on. Ask your agent
about other factors. Since the replacement value does not
include the cost of your lot, the replacement can be less than
what you paid for your home. Your personal property is covered up to certain listed limits; you should read them in
your policy. Most people don't know what the limits are
until something happens. If you want more comprehensive
coverage on certain items, ask your agent about separate
policies. Homeowner's insurance can include personal liability, medical payments to others, and inflation escalators.
You will have to balance what coverage you want with the
coverage you can afford. There will be losses that are not
insured—like earthquake and flood—by normal homeowner's policies as well as optional coverages available for additional premiums. Renter and condominium-owner policies

can also be purchased. An umbrella policy covering personal liability above the limits of your homeowner's policy is available, business liability excluded. You have a deductible on your homeowner's policy, which means the amount of each claim you must pay.

Expect your agent to call you once every couple of years to review the insurance coverage you have in place. Remodeling, inflation, or changes in your lifestyle may mean changes in your homeowner's coverage are needed.

A Few Things to Know about Auto Insurance

The best thing to do when shopping for a car is to call your insurance agent and ask him if the car you are looking at is in the high range for coverage. Booklets are available from your agent that will show the relative number of claims made for injury, collision, and theft for most cars. Given two cars, the one with the higher sticker price will have a higher premium for the same coverage. Given two identical cars with identical coverage, the one driven by a teenage boy will have a higher premium. Your policy will have a deductible, or the amount of each claim you must pay. If you raise the deductible, you lower your premium.

Your policy can cover collision, liability, car rental, and towing. Look on your billing notice for a list of your coverages. If you don't understand—and most people don't—call your agent and ask him to explain it to you. As with homeowner's insurance, you will have to balance the coverage you want with the coverage you can afford.

Mutual companies actually refund dividends if there are fewer claims. This happened in 1993 because the economy was slow and people were driving less.

Looking Ahead

Estate Planning

It is somewhat of a stretch to include a discussion of estate planning in this book because the problems resulting from poor estate planning usually don't come up until after *both* spouses die. However, enough widows have said to me, "I wish we had taken care of this before my husband died," so I have included a few reminders, if only to give peace of mind to the surviving spouse.

Make an appointment with a qualified estate attorney. If you have an estate worth less than $600,000 and your affairs and family situation are uncomplicated, look for an attorney who works with estates enough (about 50 percent of the time) to know how to deal with any contingencies that might arise.

If you have a larger estate, use an attorney who works with estates at least 50 percent of the time and has worked with estate audits. The IRS audits estates of $2,000,000 or more as a matter of course. The attorney you choose may work in the wills and trusts section of a large law firm or in a boutique firm that specializes in tax, trusts, estates, and corporate matters.

How much should you expect to pay the attorney? This varies by locality but should range anywhere from $115 to $250 per hour. You should expect to pay at least $300 even for a simple will. The more complicated your affairs—second families, children from prior marriages, business interests, real property, unusual bequests—the more you can expect in costs. You are paying for judgment, more than for a process. Attorneys will remind you it is a question of pay me now or pay me later. If you ignore estate planning now, the attorney will be paid to untangle your affairs later. It is easy to be pennywise and pound foolish on matters of estate planning.

When you go for the appointment with your attorney, take a copy of your current will and an up-to-date net worth statement. If you have them, take buy-sell agreements, trust documents, durable powers of attorney, and deeds. Ask the attorney what will happen under your existing documents when the first spouse dies and after the second spouse dies and what the estate taxes might be. With changes in the estate tax law and changes in family status, what you want to happen may not be what is going to happen. You may want the attorney to rewrite your will or to add codicils. You may be advised to retitle assets.

When naming guardians and trustees for your minor children, remember that the best person to raise your children may not be the person with the best money management skills; many couples name *different* individuals as guardians and as trustees. Name a successor guardian and successor trustee in case of death.

The next item of business is the durable power of attorney, the legal document that names who can act in your behalf in all matters of business should you become incapacitated. A well-prepared durable power of attorney for you and your spouse is a critical part of your estate planning package. It prevents having to initiate a time-consuming, costly conservatorship proceeding as well as the expense of paying a court-appointed conservator later and possible abuse by someone unfamiliar to you. I know a situation in which a court-appointed conservator loaned himself $250,000 from the estate of the person he was supposedly protecting. As with your wills, be sure someone knows where to locate the durable power of attorney documents.

Your health care durable power of attorney can be stand-alone or can be incorporated into your existing durable power of attorney. It names the person you wish to act on your behalf regarding medical issues, in the event of your incapacity. Statutes and court precedents authorize the use of a health care durable power of attorney as a legally acceptable document. If you have strong views about whether or not you want life-sustaining measures in the event of a terminal condition, you need to have a health care durable power of attorney. Without one you run the risk that a hospital or nursing home will be forced to provide you with life-sustaining measures in order to protect themselves from a possible lawsuit.

If the single estates of you and your spouse are worth over $600,000 each or your joint estate is over $1,200,000, estate taxes eventually will be due. Talk with your team of financial advisers about ways to generate liquidity in an illiquid estate to pay these taxes and about ways to preserve your wealth for your children. If your estate is of this size, your attorney may counsel you to retitle assets now so that each of you has enough in his or her single name to fund a $600,000 bypass trust. These trusts can be funded now or at your death. Only assets in your single name can be used to fund a trust after your death. These trusts typically pay income to the surviving spouse as needed, and the principal can be invaded for the benefit of the surviving spouse. When the surviving spouse dies, what is left in the bypass trust passes tax-free to the named remainderman. If you do not use this opportunity, you lose it and your estate may have to pay taxes that could have been avoided. It would be best to address these issues while the two of you are still alive.

FEDERAL ESTATE TAXES

Net Taxable Estate	*Federal Estate Taxes*
$600,000	$0
700,000	37,000
800,000	75,000
900,000	114,000
1,000,000	153,000
2,000,000	588,000
3,000,000	1,098,000
4,000,000	1,648,000
5,000,000	2,198,000
10,000,000	4,948,000
15,000,000	7,948,000
20,000,000	10,948,000
30,000,000	16,500,000
40,000,000	22,000,000
50,000,000	27,500,000
100,000,000	55,000,000

State inheritance taxes vary from state to state. Your local estate attorney is your best source of information.

There are self-help books on writing your own will and setting up your own trusts. To me, that is like performing your own leg amputation. If your affairs are complicated in any way, you want to pay for good advice. It will save you money and grief in the long run. If you choose to write your own will or trust, at least have it reviewed by an estate attorney in your state of residence.

Much has been written about avoiding probate. The reasons sometimes given for this are privacy, fees, and time. After your will has been filed in the probate office, anyone can read it; no one can read your trust without your permission. Fees are charged by attorneys in some states as a percentage of the probatable assets; if you live in such a state, it makes sense to keep costs down by avoiding probate. Time is a moot point; sometimes attorneys argue that the time involved in handling someone's affairs is really pretty much the same whether he or she avoids probate or not. Insurance salesmen and proponents of living trusts will argue that time involved in passing assets may be less if you don't have to go through probate. If you want to avoid probate, use insurance, jointly held assets, and living trusts.

The Living Trust

This is a trust you create and fund while you are still living. It is revocable, which means that you can take it back. The assets in the trust are included in your estate for estate tax purposes, but not for probate. The single most important reason for having a living trust is to avoid probate in a state where such costs are expensive. This is not the case in every state. Ask your attorney about the relative costs of handling a revocable trust after the deaths of husband and wife versus going through the probate process in your state.

In conjunction with a living trust, you must have a "pour over" will that states that upon your death any assets that have not been placed in your trust prior to death will be "poured over" into your trust. Inevitably there will be some forgotten asset and your estate will have to be probated, at least regarding those "found" assets.

Just as with a will, you should review your trust periodically to update for changes in your family or changes in the tax law.

A bank or brokerage firm can hold your trust assets for you or you can hold them yourself.

The individual reports all trust income on his tax return, just as he did when the assets were titled in his name. The tax number of the revocable living trusts is the taxpayer's Social Security number. In 1981 Congress passed a law stating that a *separate* return need not be filed for a revocable trust.

No court action is necessary to terminate a living trust. Since it is revocable, you can take all the assets back into your own name.

The attorney who draws up your living trust should be experienced sufficiently in trusts to handle all contingencies. Use the same guidelines you would use for hiring an estate attorney—choose one who spends at least 50 percent of the time handling trusts and estates.

Trust Departments

The decision to name or not name a trust department as corporate trustee in one's will is made while both spouses are doing their estate planning. Once the testator (person whose will is being written) is deceased, it can be difficult and expensive to change a named trustee. Why would your spouse name a trust department to be your trustee rather than you or an adult child? He may feel you can't handle your affairs because they are too complicated or because you lack the skill, the time, or the interest. This means you will pay a trust department at your bank or brokerage house to do it for you. For a fee, a trust department will pay your bills, make distributions to heirs, do your trust's tax return, manage and sell real property, and manage an investment portfolio. Except in unusual circumstances, it's best to give the widowed spouse some freedom to choose her own corporate trustee if she wants one and freedom to be able to change the corporate trustee. Your attorney can word the trust document to allow this freedom. Many attorneys are writing wills now with break clauses to make it less expensive and easier to "fire" a trust department that does not perform to your satisfaction. Should you and your spouse decide to name a corporate trustee in your wills, you should include a break clause.

A trust department isn't required. A bank, insurance company, or brokerage house can hold the trust assets as they would any other holding. You or any other adult can serve as trustee.

Business Continuation

Partnerships and Private Corporations

Some of the hardest problems for a widow to solve are those relating to her husband's closely held business. When your husband dies, who is the new partner? You are. If you did not contribute and if he had been a major contributor in the past to the cash flow of the business, there may be a great resentment to your taking an equal share of the profits, even if you are an equal partner. There could be even greater resentment and conflict if you step in and try to participate as a partner in a business in which you have no skills or knowledge. These problems can be solved by business owners and their spouses reaching a buy-sell agreement for disposition of the business upon death of a partner. This will be a written legal document signed by all owners. Having an agreement is one thing; funding it is another. It does no good to have a buy-sell agreement if there is no money behind it. Commonly, the partners own life insurance policies on each other in the amount of the agreed-upon buyout. When a partner dies, the proceeds are used to purchase the widow's share. Alternatively a portion of the company's assets can be set aside to repurchase stock from the widow. Be sure to reevaluate the business periodically and upgrade the insurance and agreement. If your husband dies when his company is doing well you don't want to be paid what his share was worth five years ago!

Sole Ownerships

What if your spouse is the sole owner of the business? Be sure the two of you have discussed with your banker what the business's credit will be should something happen to your spouse. If your spouse is responsible for a large portion of the cash flow, your banker may not see your business without your spouse as the same business it was with him. Will notes be called in if your husband dies, forcing a sale of the business? If you have one or more children who expect to continue or assume positions in the family business after your spouse's death, great care is needed. Those decisions should be made by the business owners before the need arises. If you have children who do not participate in the family business and some who do, you and your spouse should work out in writing how to compensate them. This can prevent some conflict in the family when your spouse dies and you are not in a frame of mind to deal with it. If neither you nor your children are interested in running the business after your spouse's death, put a manager in line *before* the need arises. If you do not wish to own the business, while your spouse is still alive you might reach an agreement with employees or third parties to buy the business from you after his death. If it is not possible to sell the business, then all you can do is be sure your spouse has left you a list of possible buyers of assets and equipment.

I cannot emphasize how important it is for you to attend to these matters while your husband is alive. You will not be in a frame of mind to handle these things after his death or disability. Employees will sense that things are up in the air and may leave. Whether or not the business is to be sold, you want "business as usual" to continue.

Conclusion

Today men will die, divorce their wives, or become disabled. There are women who will suffer financially from these events because they weren't prepared. Don't let this happen to you.

There are men and women who are reluctant to share financial facts with each other. This book has given you some techniques for breaking through that reluctance. Use the step-by-step guide to financial organization in thirty days outlined in this book. The notebook you prepare by using these steps will be a valuable tool in your financial self-defense.

Put in place your strategies for defending yourself financially. Use the knowledge you've gained about dealing with the system, budgeting and saving, divorce, investments, insurance, financial accounts, estate planning, and business continuation.

Good luck!

Bibliography

Abts, Henry W. *The Living Trust.* Chicago: Contemporary Books, 1989.

Armstrong, Alexandra, and Mary Donahue. *On Your Own: A Widow's Passage to Emotional and Financial Well-Being.* Chicago: Dearborn Financial Publishing, 1993.

Bach, George R., and Peter Wyden. *The Intimate Enemy: How to Fight Fair in Love and Marriage.* New York: Avon Books, 1968.

Beattie, Melody. *Codependent No More.* San Francisco: HarperCollins, 1981.

Berger, Esther. *Money Smart: Secrets Women Need to Know about Money.* New York: Simon & Schuster, 1993.

Bilodeau, Lorraine. *The Anger Workbook.* Minneapolis: CompCare Publishers, 1992,

Briles, Judith. *Financial Savvy for Women: A Money Book for Women of All Ages.* New York: Master Media Limited, 1992.

Dinkmeyer, Don, and Jon Carlson. *Time for a Better Marriage.* Circle Pines, Minn.: American Guidance Service, 1984.

Glasser, William. *Control Theory: A New Explanation of How We Control Our Lives.* New York: Harper & Row, 1984.

Jones-Lee, Anita. *Women and Money: A Guide for the '90's.* Hauppage, N.Y.: Barron's Educational Services, 1991.

Lerner, Harriet G. *The Dance of Anger: A Woman's Guide to Changing the Patterns of Intimate Relationships.* New York: Harper & Row, 1985.

Lerner, Harriet G. *The Dance of Intimacy: A Woman's Guide to Courageous Acts of Change in Key Relationships.* New York: Harper & Row, 1989.

Lynch, Peter. *Beating the Street.* New York: Simon & Schuster, 1993.

Lynch, Peter. *One Up on Wall Street.* New York: Viking Press, 1989.

Quinn, Jane Bryant. *Everybody's Money Book.* New York: Delacorte Press, 1979.

Quinn, Jane Bryant. *Making the Most of Your Money.* New York: Simon & Schuster, 1991.

White, Shelby. *What Every Woman Should Know about Her Husband's Money.* New York: Random House, 1992.